BOXERS
TODAY

WITHDRAWN

JO ROYLE

RINGPRESS

Published by Ringpress Books Ltd,
Spirella House, Bridge Road,
Letchworth, Herts, SG6 4ET

Discounts available for bulk orders
Contact the Special Sales Manager at
the above address. Telephone (0462) 674177

First Published 1993

ISBN 0 948955 08 2

Printed and bound in Singapore
by Kyodo Printing Co

CONTENTS

DEDICATION

To my friend "Cookie" – Mrs Cooke of the Greentubs Boxers who befriended me and helped me so much in the early days. And to the Boxers: Sterling – still my one and only – Cha Cha, Clapper, Drama, Peko, Liza, Chippy, Melba and Gracie, who took me to shows where we won so many prizes, and who gave me so much love and devotion.

Onstage Fair Dinkum.
Pearce.

ACKNOWLEDGEMENTS

My thanks to Millicent Ingram and her daughter, Ann, for the loan of the scrapbooks with *Our Dogs* and *Dog World* Boxer Breed Notes from 1936 onwards – marvellous, but such time-wasters! To Sue Drinkwater for her interest and for the use of 'Boss' for the jacket photography. To John Farrell for lending me books – how I wish I could read German!

For help with photographs, I would like to thank Helen and Eddie Banks, John and Mary Hambleton, Joy Malcolm, Lyn and Peter Durkin, Anne and Bill Law, Walker and Yvonne Miller, Margaret and Frank Wildman, Annabel and Vince Zammit, John and Linda Carnaby and John Thomson. Special thanks are due to Alessandro Tanoni for the beautiful photographs of Italian boxers from the Colle Dell Infinito. Thanks to Billie McFadden for help with America, and to Richard Tomita for the lovely photographs of American Jacquet Boxers. Thanks to Robert McDougal for listening and being at the end of the telephone, and to Peter for his typing and encouragement. If he had not nagged me this book would not even have been started, let alone finished. Finally, many thanks to Julia Barnes for dragging it all together and being so patient with me!

INTRODUCTION

It was in the mid-1950s that I first became interested in Boxers. In July 1952 my much-loved, poor-quality Indian Boxer whelped four pups. Two years later in 1954, her only daughter whelped seven puppies. I thought that one of these did not look like the others in the litter, so I thought it was the best! Mrs Cooke of the Greentubs Boxers, the owner of the sire, was asked to come and see the litter, and after a very keen, close look, said that there was one that was not at all bad: "Yes" I said, "I know, and I am going to show him!" Six months later, 'Cookie' saw him again. She was non-committal, and she asked me if I knew what showing was like. I had been to two shows, once with my aunt, who was showing her Chow, and once to watch the Boxers, so, of course, I knew all about dog shows! Cookie snorted and began to start to put me wise.

There was an Open Show at Harrow, quite close, so I sent for a schedule and entered. On the day of the show, I arrived several hours early at the hall (I never did that again!); my dark brindle Boxer had a new, very broad white show lead (afterwards I threw that away!), and shaking in my shoes, I went into the ring with my Boxer and he won a second prize, so I collected 15 shillings with my beloved Onstage Sterling Silver. I was hooked!

By the next year, Sterling went Best of Breed at the London Bullbreeds Club Show. Two years later, we went to our first Championship Show, where Fred Cross was judging Boxers, and Sterling won the Limit Class, and so won his way into the Kennel Club Stud Book, winning £2. Unfortunately my wallet was stolen, and so I lost my winnings. After that I stopped keeping accounts, because I began travelling long distances to get to shows, and I have never dared to keep accounts since!

I was extremely lucky to meet Mrs Cooke. She took me under her wing and guided me through the quagmire of Boxer showing. She gave me advice and shared with me her many years of experience in the dog business. Cookie and I travelled all over the country to shows. In those days the motor car was still a bit primitive and

Jo Royle and one of the more recent members of the Onstage Boxers.

some of our journeys were extremely hairy. A great deal more use was made, by dogs and dog people, of the train because of the difficulties of long-distance travel, both for going to shows and for sending bitches for stud. Chester Championship Show was geared to the railway timetable as the first classes used to start at 12 noon, after the London train had arrived! If we went as far afield as Scotland, that entailed an overnight stop.

On many of these journeys, Cookie would ask me what I thought of some of the winning dogs, and asked me the reason for my views, always guiding me back to the Standard and reminding me that it was not my opinion that mattered, but how close to the Standard the dogs were. It was the Standard that mattered all the time, and not our individual interpretation of the Standard. It was through Cookie, who was the breeder of Ch. Panfield Party Piece of Greentubs, that I came to know Dibby Somerfield, who was a great character, had a wonderful true eye for a dog, and a gorgeous sense of humour. Cookie was also a great friend of Connie Wiley, and whenever there was an exciting litter at Wardrobes, it was essential for a novice like me to accept an invitation and go over and have a look.

This was a marvellous era, full of personalities, and some memorable dogs. The show scene has changed a great since then – not always for the better. However, we all share a true passion for our marvellous breed – the Boxer.

Chapter One

ORIGINS OF THE BREED

THE BIRTH OF DOG BREEDS

The Boxer that we know today is almost exactly one hundred years old. The breed was evolved around the Munich area in Southern Germany, by a group of German gentlemen who were involved with a small type of Bull-baiting dog found all over Europe in the second half of the 1800s. The exact date of birth of the first Boxer is 1895.

The detailed origins of the dog do not have a place in a book on present-day Boxers, but we should never forget that the ancestor of all breeds of dog is descended from the wolf. At some time in the very distant past, the wolf found suitable food close to man's habitation – possibly man's leftovers. Man found that the wolf was fast and could catch prey quickly and easily. The wolf was able to scent and so could find the prey; it was brave and had sharp teeth – a ready-made tool. So a practical companionship developed between man and wolf.

Eventually, man was able to harness the wolf's shape and natural instincts to his (man's) advantage, so gradually, over time, different wolf/dog types evolved. Long-legged animals were mated together for a fast hunting type to catch the prey. Slower, larger animals were mated, and their offspring left behind as guards of family and compound, while the hunters were away. And the smaller animals, probably the runts of the litter, became the 'hot-water bottles' for man: cuddling up to a creature that was always warmer must have been a great comfort!

This early like-to-like breeding, which I am sure was deliberate, was how dog breeding started, and eventually specific breeds or 'breed-types' evolved. The heavily-wooded European continent, with its large forest clearings, demanded a slightly different type of hunting dog. The dog did not need to be quite so fast, but strong and agile enough to take down boars, bears and wild pigs – the slower wild beasts. These dogs had to be very brave and cunning, learning how to avoid being caught by tusks and horns, and they had to be shorter in the leg to be able to duck under the head of the beast. So, eventually, the slower, guard dogs came into their own; the small Mastiff type of dog was cultivated and very much prized.

The Romans were very keen on this Mastiff type of dog, particularly those found in Europe and Britain. The English 'Doggen' is mentioned in manuscripts and shown in early illustrations. In fact, this was the start of animal husbandry. Breeding of all animals, including dogs, began to be taken seriously, and we 'stockmen' became increasingly important members of society.

BULL-BAITING

Beasts were now being bred for meat for human consumption, and slaughtered by butchers. The small Mastiff type of dog was no longer needed to catch the beasts. However, it was thought that the meat would be more tender if it came from a beast when it was angry, when "its blood was up". So butchers kept their own dog or a couple of dogs, which were set on the tethered beast to bait it before it was slaughtered. This is how the 'sport' of Bull-baiting began. Butchers sometimes had a small piece of land near their shop where the bull or beast was tethered to a ring for this barbaric sport to take place. Sometimes the village green or town square was used. The Bullring in Birmingham, UK, is called after a place of ritual killing.

All over Europe, Bull-baiting was considered a sport, and there was also a very practical reason for it. The noise of the dogs and the bull during the baiting could be heard for miles around, and customers would know when fresh meat was available. I understand that traditionally Tuesdays and Thursdays were the days to buy your meat! Other dogs in the neighbourhood naturally heard what was going on, so trotted along to join in the fun, often bringing their owners with them, or anyone else who was interested. The dog-owning general public thought that their dogs would be as good at baiting as those of the butcher, so set them on to the bull, laying bets on the outcome – how long could the dog hold on to the enraged bull, or how far could the bull toss the dog away!

Gambling was a way of life in the 16th and 17th century. Wagers were laid for all kinds of reasons, some quite disgusting. Dog fighting, cock fighting, putting a terrier into a 'pit' of rats, bear-baiting, as well as bull-baiting, were all considered 'spectator sports' and the spectators were encouraged to gamble as part of the entertainment. These 'sports' were banned by law around 1865, and the butcher's dog reverted back to being a guard of the premises and a family pet.

Over the years, the companionship between man and dog developed, and few expeditions set off overseas without some canine companions. The bones of a small dog were recently found with those of a sailor in the Tudor warship, the *Mary Rose* – a sailor's little comforter! In those days, there were few travel restrictions, as for

Bull-baiting took place all over Europe, with most butchers keeping a couple of dogs to bait the beast before it was slaughtered.

Bull-baiting soon developed into a spectator sport, and gambling on the result was encouraged as part of the entertainment.

many years there had been wars all over Europe. Many of the fighting men were either mercenaries or troops fighting for their own countries. All these armies had their camp-followers, in many cases four-legged ones. It is well-documented that at Badajos in the Peninsular War in 1812, some of the officers had a pack of English Fox Hounds and some Greyhounds to catch hares to supply them with fresh food. So no doubt there was the odd bull-baiting dog amongst those very important camp-followers.

Packs of bull-baiting dogs were still being used to hunt boars and wild pigs in the forests of Germany and in the Austrian areas of Europe. The local names for this small Mastiff type of dog were Barenbeiser, Bullenbeiser, Brabanter and Danziger. Many of the large houses, castles and estates had their own packs of this type of dog. As they were kept in packs they naturally bred together, so that breeds started to evolve. The intelligence and character of the Mastiff type was thought to be exceptional by all those who came into contact with them, and eventually in the 1880s a few men, who particularly admired this type of dog, got together in Munich to try and establish a super-breed.

THE FIRST BOXER CLUB
I like to think of this band of enthusiasts meeting in some beer house with their mugs of beer in front of them, their dogs curled up under the table snoozing quietly while the 'master fanciers' talked over the traits they wanted, or already had, in this super-breed. They were very well organised, taking copious notes. They decided they would keep a record book, giving each dog a number, writing down details of each dog and its breeding, keeping a note of the good points and the bad points, and which of these points should be passed on, and which were undesirable and should be eliminated. This book eventually became the Stud Book of the Munich, and then the German Boxer Club. I understand that records of breeding and pedigrees were being kept for some packs of Foxhounds in the UK at this time, but there do not appear to be any records of other breeds until much later.

LECHNER'S BOXEL
In 1887, one of these Boxer fanciers, George Alt, went to France and brought back to Munich a dark brindle and white bitch. He called her 'Flora'. She probably looked very like the dogs that he and his friends found so interesting and were keen to breed. Flora had no pedigree; in fact, her parentage was unknown. In Munich, Flora was mated to one of the dogs from a pack kept locally. One of the puppies, a white, from the resulting litter was acquired by Herr Lechner, and so came to be known as Lechner's Boxel. I imagine that Herr Lechner lived in or had connections with a town or village called Boxel. Possibly the dog came from a pack from the village of Boxel, or even Boxtel. The dog's name was later shortened to Box.

It is important to bear in mind that these events occurred a very long time ago, and surviving records are sketchy, so it is a matter of speculating and piecing together a few known facts. An unknown pedigree is exactly that. Documents have not been lost – there have been no documents at all. No-one knew who the parents were, and I suspect, sometimes no-one knew where that dog had been born.

We now have some very close breeding, presumably to try to 'fix' what these fanciers were looking for. George Alt put Flora, the brindle and white French bitch,

Alt's Schecken: A white bitch with brindle patches, the result of a mating between Lechner's Box (all-white) and Alt's Flora, his mother, (dark brindle). She was to become the mother of Flocki, the first Boxer.

back to her son, Lechner's Box. The result was a litter born in November 1893, in which there was a white bitch puppy with brindle patches. George Alt kept her, and she became known as Alt's Schecken.

New blood was needed, so it was fortunate that around this time a Dr Toenissen joined the group of fanciers. Dr Toenissen owned an English Bulldog, which some records tell us was imported from England. This dog was white with a few fawn patches, and his parentage was unknown. In those days the English Bulldog was more like the present-day Staffordshire Bull Terrier in stature, but with a short brachicephalic head, and a short blunt muzzle.

THE FIRST BOXER

The predominantly white English Bulldog was mated to the in-bred, mostly white, Alt's Schecken, and on February 26th 1895, Flocki was born. Flocki was written down as Number 1 in the German Munich Stud Book. So Flocki was the very first Boxer! Flocki's parents were white or predominantly white; he was a dark brindle with flashy white markings. Both his front legs were white, and he had a white blaze and a white muzzle. He certainly looks all Boxer – how well I recognise that keen, stubborn, enquiring look!

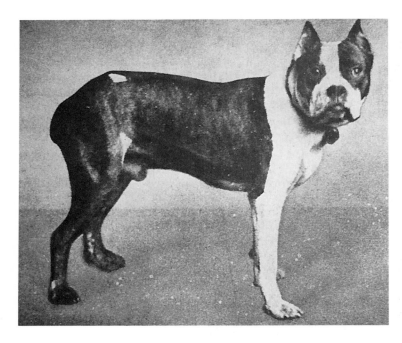

Flocki ZB No. 1: The first Boxer registered in the German Munich Stud Book. He was born in 1895, sired by Tom the Bulldog out of Alt's Schecken (both predominantly white).

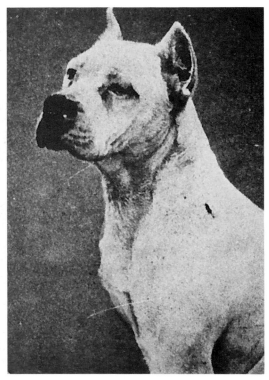

Piccolo v. Argentor: Sired by Maier's Lord (brindle) out of Maier's Flora (white). He was to become the sire of Meta v.d. Passage, the foundation bitch of the Boxer breed when mated to another pure white Boxer, Ch. Blanca v Argentor.

Ch. Blanka v. Argentor showing the size and build of the early Boxers.

Ch. Blanka v. Argentor: The result of a repeat mating between Tom the Bulldog and Alt's Flora. Although her parents had very un-Boxer-like heads, they produced a very typical Boxer-headed daughter.

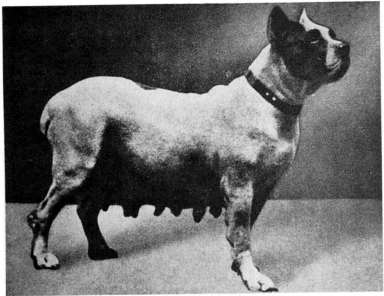

Meta v.d. Passage (Piccolo v. Argentor – Blanka v. Argentor): Born in 1898, this lightly marked pale fawn bitch had an tremendous influence on the development of the breed. She produced three dominant stud dogs (by different sires), and these bloodlines spread worldwide.

Hugo v. Pfalzgau (Flock St Salvator – Meta v.d. Passage): Born in 1900, this dark fawn dog appears in many important pedigrees worldwide, and it is claimed that many Boxers are descended from him.

Flocki ZB No. 1 is listed in some records as Muhlbauer's Flocki, so I assume Flocki belonged to Herr Muhlbauer, one of the early Boxer fanciers. At all events, Flocki went on to win the Boxer class put on at a St Bernard Show (which was the reason he earned the Number 1 spot in the Boxer Stud Book), and so a repeat mating was planned between Tom, the Bulldog, and Alt's Schecken. This time they

Girgel (Wotan – Meta v.d. Passage): Born in 1901, this brindle dog was used extensively at stud.

Schani v.d. Passage (Flock St Salvator – Meta v.d. Passage): Born in 1902, this very pale fawn dog was the third of Meta's sons who became a dominant stud dog.

produced a pure white bitch, who, much later, became Ch. Blanka von Argentor.

Meanwhile, Lechner's Box and Alt's Flora had produced a brindle dog, who was called Maier's Lord, who, when mated to his kennel companion, Maier's Flora (a white), produced Piccolo von Argentor, a pure white dog. Blanka von Argentor and Piccolo von Argentor, both pure whites, were then mated, and their daughter was a

Some of the early Boxer fanciers pictured at the first Boxer show on March 29th 1896.

lightly marked pale fawn. This bitch, Meta von der Passage, became one of the great Boxer producers of all time. So it seems that it is a little hard to blame Tom the Bulldog for the white puppies we still get in many of our litters today!

I have been concentrating on this very close early breeding because Meta von der Passage is widely known as the foundation of all Boxers, the Boxer 'Eve', as it were. Actually, I think the true foundation bitch was Flora, the bitch imported from France by George Alt, which certainly raises the question of the breed's German origins. However, Meta von der Passage certainly had a tremendous influence on Boxers, even those of today. Through her several matings, Meta was the mother of three early stud dogs, and so was able to influence the whole Boxer breed. As a result of the chaos of two World Wars, the breeding of these three dogs was spread worldwide.

One mating was to Flock St Salvator (not to be confused with Flocki, the first Boxer). Flock St Salvator was born in March 1894 and was a light fawn. His father was Box St Salvator. Box was also a light fawn, and was of unknown parentage, as was Flock's mother, Mary von Nymphenburg. Meta and Flock were the parents of Schani von der Passage (a very light fawn dog), Schlag Bitru (a brindle dog) and Hugo von Pfalzgau (a dark fawn dog). All these three dogs were well used stud dogs and good producers, although Hugo von Pfalzgau appears in the most important

A group of Boxers at the 1896 Boxer show.

pedigrees. Meta von der Passage was then mated to Wotan, whose breeding is a bit suspect. His sire, Nero Ascenbrenner, was of unknown parentage, but with a name like Nero, it might be surmised that he was dark in colour. Wotan's dam was Weber's Ella, a fawn, sired by Maier's Sultan out of Frey's Nelly. As these two are named after two of the early fanciers, it is probably safe to assume that they were good-quality Boxers or good-quality Boxer types. This mating of Meta and Wotan produced Girgel.

Wotan was also mated to Mirzel, a fawn grand-daughter of Lechner's Box and Alt's Flora; they also produced a son, Moritz von Pfalhau. The Meta sons, Girgel, Hugo von Pfalzgau, Moritz von Pfalzgau, and Meta herself, were great-great-grandparents of Rolf von Vogelsberg, a marvellous Boxer, who won at shows all over Europe. Eventually, in 1911, Rolf came into the hands of a newly married Friederun, who had just become the wife of Philip Stockmann. Rolf von Vogelsberg was the apple of Friederun's eye, and she showed him fearlessly everywhere. He became her top-winning Boxer, and he was the father of the first 'von Dom' Boxers. Boxers from that strain are still remembered and much admired, and the breeding is valued all over the world.

Friederun and Philip Stockmann were both artists and had the true artist's eye for a dog, and particularly for the Boxer. Friederun's sculptures of her Boxers and their puppies just ooze the essence of the Boxer, as do the delightful pen-and-ink doodles of her dogs in the margin of her unforgettable book *My Life with Boxers*, the biography of her kennel of Boxers and her life with them. Her husband, Philip, was involved with the Munich Boxer Club and then the German Boxer Club. Later he was the Chief Warden for Boxers in Germany, and wrote definitive articles for the club magazine *Boxer Blatter*, as well as many general articles on the breed, which to this day we still prize, regarding them as no less than Boxer Law.

Chapter Two

THE BOXER IN GERMANY

CH. ROLF VON VOGELSBERG

I consider that for a dog to be called 'great', it has to have some lasting influence on a breed, and there also has to be someone to record that influence. Rolf von Vogelsberg was lucky in that he was a great favourite of Frau Stockmann, and he features in her delightful book *My Life with Boxers*, now unfortunately out of print. I am going to concentrate on Rolf because he was an important influence both in Germany and the whole continent of Europe. America was just discovering the breed, and many of Rolf's children and grandchildren, mostly of the von Dom affix, were exported to the USA. Later on, through American imports, Rolf also became an influence in Britain.

Rolf von Vogelsberg was line-bred to the great Meta von der Passage, who was his grandmother on both his father's and his mother's side. Rolf was sired by Curt von Pfalzgau, who was, in turn, the grandson of Meta von der Passage and Flock St Salvator. On his dam's side, Venus von Vogelsberg was the great-grand-daughter of Meta when mated to Wotan. So when Rolf joined the von Dom kennel, he brought a great deal of the original Boxer breeding to Friederun Stockmann's Boxers.

Friederun Stockmann probably knew the Rolf von Vogelsberg story better than anyone, and she gives a full account in her book. In those early days, many lucky accidents seemed to occur, and it was certainly good fortune that Rolf von Vogelsberg joined the von Dom kennel – good fortune for him and for all of us involved with Boxers. Friederun saw Rolf at her first big dog show, and it was love at first sight. Eventually she was able to buy him, and he became her proudest and most cherished possession. Friederun understood him so well, and in turn, he was devoted to her.

Friederun writes in her book: "In the year 1910, Rolf was shown for the first time in Darmstadt, and he went straight to the top. Following that success, in the same year, he won the Champion Medal in Dresden, Wursburg, Nuremberg and Chemnitz,

Bosko v. Immegrun and the puppy, Don Juan v. Immergrun. This line leads directly to Rolf v. Volgelsberg, who brought a great deal of original Boxer breeding to the von Dom Boxers.

Frau Stockmann at home feeding her Boxers. Ch. Rolf v. Vogelsberg is pictured on the extreme right. This photograph was taken before Rolf and Philip Stockmann went to war in 1914.

thus becoming a full Champion. Further shows brought victory after victory. When he came home after the war at eleven years of age, he won his fifth and last Challenge Certificate.

"Rolf was bred by Mr Brechtel, a veterinary surgeon in Codalzburg, near Furth. He was sold when he was half-grown, but did not get into the right hands. He was given too much freedom, and was on the way to becoming useless, when Dr Schulein saw him in the street one day, and immediately bought him for a ridiculously low price. The Doctor was an expert on dogs and knew full well that he had just purchased a valuable animal.

"However Rolf set his new master many problems. He was a very bad eater, and he was always criticised at shows for being too thin. About fourteen days before a show he was fed with four pieces of cake every afternoon (in this instance 'cake' probably means dog biscuit). This was found to be the only way to get him into condition.

"Rolf was two years old when Dr Schulein bought him, and although dogs were the Doctor's hobby, he really did not have enough time to spend on them. One or two things were missing for the right doggy surroundings. When I bought Rolf he was three years old. He was still thin, but, for those days, he was a large dog, with good depth of chest and great nobility. Breeders complained, however, that their bitches often 'missed' to him, and that his puppies were difficult to rear. I wanted to alter this!

"When Dr Schulein delivered the dog to me, I was told that Rolf had vomited a stone as large as a walnut. Veterinary surgeons discovered that this stone had been in the stomach for at least a month, a conclusion based on the acid state of the stomach. Also I wormed him as soon as he came to me. In those days there was a worm cure on the market called 'Walker's Sixty Minute Cure'. For years I have been sorry that this cure has been discontinued, as I think it has never been equalled. Rolf had the 'Sixty Minute Cure' and the results were astonishing. I never thought a dog could carry so many worms inside him. After worming, all complaints about Rolf von Vogelsberg's progeny being delicate, and his sub-fertility ended."

It is very interesting to note that Frau Stockmann, writing almost a hundred years ago, is so like us Boxer breeders today. Perhaps I should say how like her we still are – slightly apprehensive of the vet's diagnosis about the stone, a great believer in her worm cure, and then being so cross that it was unobtainable!

Friederun bought Rolf about two weeks after she and Philip got married. She writes: "I was in no hurry to furnish our new home. I would rather invest the money in dogs, and I wanted to spend a thousand marks to purchase Rolf ..... my capital was just a thousand marks! I spent it all on Rolf and the financial question was resolved." I am glad to say that Philip and Friederun Stockmann lived happily ever after – another great stroke of luck in the Boxer story.

THE FIRST VON DOM CHAMPION

As a new, now wealthy, keen breeder and exhibitor, Friederun soon found that she was becoming a dumping ground for Boxer bitches – non-producers, difficult whelpers and veterans – "so very soon I had six bitches of varying ages, all to be put, hopefully, to Rolf."

In 1912 the von Dom breeding began in earnest. Rolf von Vogelsberg was the sire of two top-quality puppies, Derby and Dampf von Dom. These were the first to put the von Dom kennel on the map. In 1913 four of their Boxers were entered at Mainz show, and there were prizes for all of them. There were more wins for them that year at Karlsruhe, and at Berlin in November.

On March 4th 1914, a daughter was born to Philip and Friederun Stockmann, just as the new show season was about to start. Friederun was unable to leave the new baby to attend the big, important show in Hamburg, which was held on March 21st and 22nd. However, Philip was given strict instructions, and allowed to take the dogs to the show.

"I told my husband exactly what to do, and what not to do. He took three dogs with him, and each dog had to be handled differently. I also told him if he could get a really good price for them, he could sell two, but Dampf's fawn sister must stay in our kennel, as, under no circumstances, would I part with her."

"I sat at home waiting. Every hour I thought of my husband, and wondered what he was doing at that particular moment. At last came the time when the train was due at Bruck. Only a few minutes and my husband would be home. Then I saw him coming through the bushes, having taken a short-cut. Next to him shone a red-fawn coat. That was Derby, Dampf's sister, and then came running a small neat brindle animal. That was Urschi. Where was Dampf?

"I did not let my husband speak before I questioned him. He could only answer 'Sold'. That is how I knew that Dampf had won the title of Champion!"

This was the first home-bred von Dom Champion – the realisation of Friederun's greatest dream. Her reaction to the sale is interesting: "I congratulated my husband on his first home-bred Champion. He had been offered thirteen hundred marks for him. He knew how necessary the money was for us to make our plans come true, and he had therefore sold our first Champion. I knew he had done right, but I felt a sharp pang in my heart. So much love, so much work and sacrifice for just a handful of money!"

We now follow Dampf's long and slow journey across the Atlantic – there was no handy jumbo jet in those days. I see from the American Boxer Club's 50th Anniversary album, that 'the first Boxer to finish a Championship, was Sieger Dampf von Dom, who was made up in 1915.' His new owners were Governor and Mrs Lehman. He was the Governor of New York. The Lehmans had been Boxer fans for many years, and were early members of the American Boxer Club. Unfortunately, Dampf had no influence on American Boxers, because there were very few bitches for breeding. It was not until the early thirties that the Boxer really started to catch on in the USA.

Frau Stockmann has a final word about the Dampf sale episode – "I soon got over it. Dampf, after all, was not an improvement on his father. He was a nice dog, but I felt sure it would be possible to breed a better one."

She adds an amusing footnote to her account of the Hamburg show. "My husband told me of the trouble that he had had with the three dogs. Derby constantly jumped up on him. Dampf had not been so bad, but when it came for a special prize, Urschi had her tongue hanging out! She had never done such a thing before all the time we had her, and after the Hamburg show, it never happened again. On the day, however, the judge must have thought that she was a born tongue-shower and therefore gave the prize to her opponent, a fawn bitch that was nowhere as good as she. That is how we lost all the prize money, which incidentally, was never paid out in any case, for this prize money became with other things, a casualty of the war and inflation."

Sometime later Friederun Stockmann attended the Ulm show on July 26th 1914. She writes: "Several of the leading dogs were missing from this show. It was my intention to buy a good bitch for Rolf as the right mate for him. Just as I was making my purchase, disturbing leaflets were handed out, and everyone got restless. A month before, Archduke Ferdinand Franz and his wife had been murdered by a Serb. Austria had given Serbia an ultimatum which Serbia rejected, and the Austrian declaration of war was inevitable. Germany had declared her solidarity with Austria. This news shocked the foundations of our existence, and it was days before I really understood what was happening around me. Everything was overshadowed by the thought that my husband would become a soldier and that I would be left alone with our small child and our pack of dogs!"

WARTIME: 1914-1918

Philip Stockmann was called up by the autumn of that year. His last words to his wife were 'I know you will manage'. "This was not an empty compliment," she wrote, "but an honest conviction that came from the heart." I bet it was! Friederun Stockmann was an indomitable woman, and I am sure she could cope with any situation. She certainly managed to sustain the Boxer breed, and was quick to see how the dogs could be put to use. Ten of her Boxers went to war with Philip, accompanied by several from the County Group of the Munich Boxer Club (who campaigned to mobilise all suitable Boxers for war work). Philip had transferred to the Home Guard, in order to organise the military deployment of these dogs.

"Naturally, he much preferred this work as we both thought how much our life was happily connected with dogs. My husband had gathered a few people around him who loved and understood animals. Many Boxers would, in any case, have become homeless as their owners had been called up or were afraid that they would not be able to feed them. In those days we got a lot of dogs from kennels that could no longer feed them. Lots of them, however, were beloved by their masters, but for the love of the Fatherland, they were given up to protect husbands and sons who were risking their lives in the front lines."

Within a few months, we are told, Philip Stockmann and his brigade of dogs were in the 'front line'. "The Munich Group had collected sixty Boxers, all of whom had been given to the Army Command without payment. The Group gave each dog a collar with a strong lead ..... After our Boxers had done pioneering work, many other breeds were taken on. The organisation for War dogs had become a big thing."

The years of the Great War, 1914 to 1918, slowed down some Boxer activities, but, on reflection, these years gave a chance to once again consolidate the breeding in the areas of Southern Germany. Enthusiasts had to resort to close line breeding, because of the difficulties of travelling any distance. A few dog shows did take place, but Friederun felt that they were hardly worth attending, due to the poor competition. She spent most of her time keeping her dogs in good condition, and supplying suitable Boxers for Philip and his war dog brigade, where he and his band of animal loving handlers were being most successful.

"At first," Friederun tells us, "Boxers were attached to communication patrols behind the front lines. Their work was to ensure that prisoners of war did not receive any information from civilians, and most important of all, that they were not armed. The dogs soon learned what was required of them. When a civilian came too near a prisoner, his every move was watched closely by the dogs. That, as a rule, usually did the trick, for the dogs looked far from friendly."

Philip told his wife of the co-operation between man and dog. When on guard to watch for smugglers ('smugglers' was the word used; I suppose that it was tempting to steal rations and possibly arms found near the soldiers, which would have been useful to civilians), Philip was always able to see from the attitude of his dog (usually Rolf), when danger was at hand. The dog was always more alert when a stranger came close. When that person was a friend or German soldier, the dog's tail would wag, but if that person was not recognised, the tail would remain rigid – no wag at all! Rolf's growl was so low that Philip was only able to feel it when he put his hand on the dog's head.

When smugglers were about, they could be seen walking in single file. Rolf would watch them keenly, and when he switched his gaze back to the leader, Philip knew that was the signal to loose the dog because all had passed. In a month, Philip and Rolf were responsible for catching two hundred of these smugglers. This shows how the co-operation between man and dog could be put to good use.

Quite recently, I was watching an old black and white German newsreel of the Great War. A small bi-plane landed on a muddy field. Two men in uniform approached, closely followed by two dogs, loose with no leads on them. As the door of the plane opened, the men and the dogs stood waiting to be picked up. One of the dogs was a German Shepherd and the other was an excited Boxer. There was no doubting the clear silhouette of that second dog, or the attitude of the cropped Boxer, waiting to jump into that plane.

I have been told that Boxers, together with other breeds, were trained to carry telephone cables through the trenches between command posts, and so helped with communications. The end of the cable would be attached to the dog's collar, and he would be 'sent away' to where another handler would be waiting. Snipers watching would be unable to see the dogs in the semi-dark or twilight, unless the dog had white markings. This was the reason that Boxers without white coat markings were selected for this type of work. In those early days, plain Boxers without white markings were preferred in any case, but war work gave a very good practical reason for the breed to have as few white markings as possible. It is only recently that white markings have become popular with people for the show ring. In fact, white markings are discouraged for any kind of guarding work. The brindle colour is preferred, as it acts like camouflage. The white markings, incidentally, are usually in very vulnerable places: an accurate shot to the head or chest, where the white markings usually are, could prove fatal.

It was these white markings that the Munich Boxer Club decided were unacceptable in a Boxer guard dog. They tried to eliminate them, including the 'check' and completely white Boxer. This regulation was included in the second Breed Standard, which the club adopted. That was in the year 1924, when the Munich Boxer Club (later the German Boxer Club) managed to get the Boxer Breed approved as a working police dog. The excellent war service records of the Boxer during the Great War was one of the main reasons for the breed becoming an official police and guard dog. I believe, to this day, that a licence for an accredited working dog is cheaper in many countries in Europe, and as the dog licence is quite costly, this is a bonus for the breed.

THE BREED SPREADS

When hostilities ceased, British soldiers and some of their allies, the Americans, told the people back home that there was a special-looking dog, with a unique character, in Europe. So in the early 1920s, the Boxer, a breed that was barely twenty-five years old, began to spread all over the world.

All through the war, a 'breed type', had been bred intermittently within the countries which had been the source of the breed, but with the end of hostilities, travelling became much easier, and breeding really took off. The von Dom kennel was still the top kennel in Germany; their stud dogs were widely used, so that special breeding spread all over Europe. McDonald Daly writes in his book: "Through the 20s the von Dom kennel marched on to supremacy in Germany, producing Champion after Champion, and it was remarked in the mid-30s, that although only half of the registered Boxers were of the von Dom strain, almost all of the Best in Show winners and Champions were of that blood." Certainly, in the 1930s, Boxers of good quality could be seen everywhere.

In Germany, the great Rolf von Vogelsberg had returned from the front with his master after a successful war service, and before his death in 1920, he won another Championship, when he was twelve years old. Rolf's great-great-great grandson, Sigurd von Dom, a fawn, was now the top stud dog. Frau Stockmann writes: "He was a natural showman, and loved dog shows. He had a perfect body; front and hindquarters were correct, and his noble head was set on a strong elegant neck. He represented the ideal Boxer, combining strength with speed and nobility. Sigurd was a first-class dominant sire, and each of his youngsters carried his quality and type. He had more than his share of vanity, loving to be photographed, and would sit still until the camera shutter clicked, then with one jump, he would be gone. Sigurd had the good-natured Munich trait".

In my opinion, that description of Sigurd is priceless. It is like a show report on a great dog, who has been dead for over fifty years, written by the authority on the Boxer breed, who is no longer with us. I particularly like the fact about the 'Munich trait' being good-natured. Over the years, I have had the odd Boxer, nearly always a male, that has been exceptionally good-natured and rather special, a real 'thinking' dog, not quite like his peers. I like to think that this was the Munich trait!

It was about this time that Friederun received an enquiry from the USA for a fawn, mature Champion stud dog. Philip was abroad, and she had to make a decision alone. Sigurd was the only one who fitted the description, and at five years old he probably only had a few years left at stud, and it was difficult to find good pet homes for a dog of this age locally. There were other younger von Dom dogs at stud, and so Sigurd followed other Boxers across the 'Pond', where he became

Knirps v. Menchendahl: One of the German Boxers who went on to become an important stud dog in America. He was an extremely good-looking Boxer, but his colour (more than one-third white) was unacceptable from 1924.

International Champion Sigurd von Dom of Barmere. I imagine that he was the first International Champion, as he was already an Austrian Champion, and a German Champion, and very quickly became an American Champion.

He attained a lifetime record of two Best in Show awards, fifty-four Best of Breed, and forty-three Working Group wins, from 1935 when he was Best of Breed at Westminster in the Spring, to his death at twelve years of age There is a slight discrepancy about his age, as Frau Stockmann says he was five years old when he was exported, but the American Boxer Club Anniversary book states that he was four when he arrived there. However, he was a pre-potent stud, siring sixteen American Champions and ten imports. He was the leading American Boxer sire in 1936, and runner-up in 1939 and 1940, dominating every breeding programme, and founding a line that was easily recognised. He was exhibited fearlessly, and consistently won the stud dog classes, and was first in many of the veteran classes. He was the grandfather of three of the foundation sires in the USA: Dorian Marienhof of Maizelaine, imported to the US in 1937, Lustig von Dom, who followed in the same year, and later in 1940, Lustig's younger brother, Utz von Dom.

Mrs Breed, the owner of Sigurd and of the Barmere kennel, must have been delighted with her purchase from Germany! America was very fortunate to have so much of this concentrated von Dom breeding, and Britain was lucky to be able to import so much of that superbly bred stock later, after the second World War.

Meanwhile in 1934, back in Germany, there was a litter of puppies gambolling about in a puppy run at the von Dom kennels. It was the result of a double grandfather mating, by Zorn von Dom (a Sigurd son) and out of Esta von der Worm (a Sigurd daughter). There was an eye-catching golden fawn dog puppy in that litter. Friederun called him Lustig, and he was to bring great honour to his name and to the von Dom kennel, both in Germany and America.

Chapter Three

THE BOXER COMES TO BRITAIN

THE FIRST IMPORTS

A bitch, called Jondy, is recorded as being the first Boxer to set foot in Britain. She was born in 1911, and was royally bred, sired by Remus von Pfalzgau, a well-known show winner in Germany. (He was one of the Flock St Salvator – Meta von der Passage sons.) Jondy did not produce a litter, and there is no other information available about her; so she was, more than likely, someone's beloved pet. In 1919, a Dr McMaster brought a pair of Boxers to Ballymena, Northern Ireland. Little is known about them, although I understand that Allon Dawson saw them and said that they were good specimens. There are no records of them producing any Boxer puppies. In 1930, another Boxer came over to England. He was born in Paris in 1927, but again, he did not sire a litter in the UK, to our knowledge.

There was another Boxer in the UK, who was an unregistered family pet. Angela Dulante, a member of that family, later became a professional photographer, and she was the owner of Ch. Panfield Beau Jinks. I like to think that she was drawn to the breed because of the fun she had with the family pet. I understand from an article written by one of the very early pioneers of the breed, Mary Davies, that a well-illustrated article on the breed was published by the *Harmsworth Dog Encyclopaedia*, and a team of football-playing Boxers also appeared at Bertram Mills's circus. Miss Clay of the Tantivvy Dalmatians, told me of this exciting display that she and the two Miss Rogers (also in Dalmatians) enjoyed one evening, and were absolutely captivated!

At this time Miss Patience Rogers decided she had to have a Boxer, and instructed Spratts to find her a Boxer bitch in whelp. So in 1932 we have the first serious import, Cilly von Rothenberg, in whelp to Drill von Kurland. A litter was born in quarantine, but only three dog puppies survived. Mary Davies tells us that they were "monorchids or worse"! (What could be worse?) Miss Rogers kept Riverhill Rackateer. A second puppy was registered, rather hopefully, by Mrs Wills and

Captain Cleland, as Beginner of Willstud. The third puppy, Willi v. Brandenberg, was registered much later by Gore Graham, in February 1936, just in time to compete and win at Crufts that year. In the 1930s, very few Boxers had been registered at the Kennel Club, and these registrations were entered in the *Kennel Gazette,* so at least the Boxer now had official records in the UK.

Cilly was later mated back to her son, Riverhill Rackateer, and another litter was born, again producing only sons. However, this was the first British-bred litter, and the Misses Rogers became the very first Boxer breeders in the UK. Some time later Cilly von Rothenberg was acquired by Mrs Cecil Sprigge and mated to her import, Fritz of Leith Hill. They produced a daughter, Tilly of Leith Hill, who did breed on, but I can find no trace of her progeny.

At that time some other well-known breeders began to show interest in Boxers – Miss Watson (Fieldburcote), Miss Monkhouse (Cabaret), and the aforementioned Miss Clay (Tantivvy). In fact, they were all Dalmatian breeders, and clearly they appreciated an active breed like the Boxer. At this time, Bill Siggers, later one of our much-loved and expert all-rounder judges, was the kennel manager of Mr J. V. Rank's Great Dane kennel. His wife, Dulcie, became interested in the new breed, and she imported a bitch, named Anita von der Konradshone, from Munich. When this bitch was mated to Mr Rankin's Arras von Neibesheim, she produced a litter of eight. This included Cuckmere Krin, who won the first-ever Challenge Certificate awarded to a Boxer – a landmark for the breed. Other Boxer imports to come in at that time were two bitches imported by Mr Burman – Birka von Emilenhorst, and Quittas von Biederstein, who went to Mr Dawson's Stainburndorf kennel – and a dog, Brief von Kalhound, who was brought in by Mrs Sneyd.

In researching the history of the Boxer, I feel that not enough importance has been given to Mrs Cecil Sprigge of Abinger Common, Surrey, who was a great influence in the early days of the Boxer in the UK. Mrs Sprigge imported a red dog from France, whom she named Fritz of Leith Hill (which was her own prefix). Her import's father was Armin von der Haake, who won a first prize at the big Hamburg Championship show in 1929, so he was probably a good type of Boxer. I wish I knew what his son, Fritz, looked like. The next year Mrs Sprigge brought in a bitch from Holland, Karlington's Liesel, a daughter of Ch. Armin Edelbut. When mated to Fritz she produced eight puppies, which were all entered at the show put on by Charles Cruft in 1936. These were the first classes ever scheduled for the Boxer breed at a show in the UK.

Charles Cruft was a master showman, and he made a great deal of publicity out of this new breed in England. Mrs Sprigge got him interested in the Boxer, and she agreed to guarantee the classes if he scheduled Boxers at his Crufts show. In those days Charles Cruft owned Crufts, and was responsible for organising the show. Later the name was acquired by the Kennel Club, who now organise it, and Crufts has become one of the most famous dog shows in the world.

The Crufts' catalogue for 1936 still survives, and the winner of the very first class was Willi v. Brandenberg. There were two exhibitors, Mrs Grahame and Mrs Sprigge, and nine Boxers were entered. Two Boxers were 'not for competition' as they had cropped ears. They were Cilly von Rothenberg whom Mrs Sprigge had acquired from Miss Rogers, and Fritz of Leith Hill.

Of those who did compete, Willi v. Branderberg was an adult, born in July 1935, bred by Mrs Sprigge. The judge was a Chris Houlker. There were no entries for the Special Breeders Class, nor for the Team Class, but Mrs Sprigge did enter a Brace. I wonder which two she chose, and who took each of her puppies into the ring for their class? I like to think of those early enthusiasts, standing at the ringside comparing the dogs – the adult, Willi, and the six Leith Hill puppies – discussing the attributes of each one, and which one appealed, and why.

One of the early fanciers was a wealthy Yorkshireman, with big textile interests, called Allon Dawson. He had bred Pointers and Danes with some success. He became interested in Boxers in 1934, and was to become an important influence on the breed. The next year, 1935, he had purchased a Boxer bitch from Mrs Sprigge, whom he called Sally. She was to become his "devoted pal", her "charming disposition appealed to him very much", but he soon realised "that she was not quite the type that a Boxer should be, so he decided to import a few."

In 1936 significant imports came from Germany to Yorkshire. They were Rex von Durrenberg, Bessie von Trauntal, Hella von Eibe, Klasse von der Humboldtshobe, and – most important of all – Burga von Twiel. She was most important because she was in whelp to the illustrious Ch. Lustig von Dom. Von Dom breeding and the von Dom quality was on its way to the United Kingdom! In January 1937, a litter was born in quarantine kennels at Hessle, near Hull. On a cold, foggy winter morning, MacDonald Daly recalls "driving down to the kennels with Mr Dawson to examine these interesting babies". Two of these 'interesting babies' grew up to become Stainburndorf top winners. In 1939, Stainburndorf Vanda won the CC at the LKA, the first Bitch CC awarded to the breed, and later in that year, her sister, Stainburndorf Wendy won CCs at Kensington and Harrogate Championship shows, putting Boxers and the Stainburndorf Boxer kennel firmly on the map.

THE BRITISH BOXER DOG CLUB

The second half of the 1930s were significant years for the Boxer in the United Kingdom. In December of 1936, half a dozen enthusiasts met in London, and the

Ch. Horsa of Leith Hill: The first British Boxer Champion, born in 1936. A winner of CCs at Blackpool, Richmond and Kensington. Unfortunately, he died very young during the war years.

British Boxer Dog Club was founded. Mrs Sprigge was the first secretary and treasurer, and Mr McCandish was the president. An executive committee was appointed, consisting of Miss Birrell, Mr Betteridge and Mr Dawson. In the first year, the membership doubled from six to twelve, and in the next year, 1937, the club applied to the Kennel Club and was affiliated. By 1939 the Club was guaranteeing classes at Championship shows, and the Boxer breed had been granted Championship status.

SHOW WINNERS
Boxers were scheduled once again in 1937 at Crufts' Coronation show. As in the previous year, Mrs Sprigge guaranteed the Boxer classes. The number of Boxer exhibitors increased from two to seven. Mr Burman and Mrs Sprigge were responsible for four and five entries respectively. Mrs Caro, Mr Dawson, Mr Levy and Mr Whaley, each had a single entry.

The entire entry was a great improvement on the year before. The imports, Mr Burman's Quitta von Biederstein, Mrs Sneyd's Grief von Kahlgrund, and Mrs Sprigge's two (for by that time she had brought in Gretel von der Boxerstadt, who was to become an important influence on the breed, as well her earlier import Fritz of Leith Hill), all being cropped, had to be entered 'not for competition'.

In the Open class for dogs and bitches, Mr Burman's entries were Sigurd, Sigmond and Sigfried of Luckings, litter brothers born on August 11th 1936 (all sons of the imports, Tell von der Magdalenenquelle and Quitta von Biederstein). Sigurd was

Gold of Uttershill: CC winner at the Richmond Championship show in 1939. She later died in whelp. American bred, sired by Corso Uracher Wasserfall Se Sumbala out of So Se Sumbala.

later to go to Mr Betteridge, one of the founders of the British Boxer Dog Club. Mrs Caro had bought Horsa of Leith Hill from Mrs Sprigge, a dog who had been born in quarantine on July 3rd 1936, sired by Hansel von Beiderstein out of Gretel von der Boxerstadt. Mr Dawson was showing Ortrud of Leith Hill, who had been entered at the same show in 1936, and had been offered for sale.

Odin of Leith Hill, also shown the previous year, was now entered by Mr Levy, and Elsa of Leith Hill was entered by Mr Whaley. Mrs Sprigge entered Tilly, Horst and Hector of Leith Hill, the last two being litter brothers of Horsa. Mrs Sprigge had bred seven of the nine Boxers entered. Mr Burman entered his three Luckings Boxers in the Special Breeders class. There were no entries for the Brace class, but Mr Burman and Mrs Sprigge both entered a team. Unfortunately, I do not know of any of the placings. I wonder how Horsa of Leith Hill fared? After all, he was to become the first-ever Boxer Champion of Great Britain. His litter brother, Hengist, was offered for sale for £30, but there is no record as to whether he was sold.

I can find no details for Crufts 1938, but I see from Elizabeth Somerfield's book that the entries totalled 24. That same number of Boxers was entered at Crufts in 1939, and there was quite an explosion of exhibitors – 18! This time, the newly-formed British Boxer Dog Club guaranteed three classes. Three of the classes were mixed dogs and bitches – Puppy, Novice and Limit. Open was divided into an Open Dog and an Open Bitch class. Special Breeders, Brace, and Team were all mixed classes – a great improvement in the classification for the breed. There were three cropped imports entered 'not for competition' – Mr Dawson's Rex von Durrenberg and Bessie von Trauntal, and Gretel von der Boxerstadt, now owned by Mrs Gingell.

Where was Mrs Sprigge? What had happened to her? After days of searching, I have, at last, found a mention. In 1944 Mr Voss in 'Boxer Broadcasts', in *Our Dogs*, noted that "Mrs Cecil Sprigge, who is an acknowledged authority on Continental Affairs has lately been contributing some interesting articles to the *Manchester Guardian*." He did not think that Mrs Sprigge currently had any Boxers, but he goes on to say that she had imported some of the important first Boxers, and how influential she had been in the Boxer scene at the start of the breed. I heartily agree with him. I do not think that anyone did more for the Boxer than Mrs Sprigge at the very start, and we should all be very grateful to her.

At any rate, thanks to Mrs Sprigge, and all the early enthusiasts for the breed, and to their many imports, we, in the UK, had an excellent foundation to build on. British Boxer breeding should have become a force to be reckoned with. However, there was a problem – a World War was looming just around the corner.

There is an interesting and amusing insight to the start of this war which matches up with Frau Stockmann being showered by leaflets at the Ulm Dog Show, in 1914, at the outbreak of the First World War. MacDonald Daly writes: "On September 2nd, 1939, Mr Dawson and I chatted about his new dog, (that was Zuntfig von Dom), at Harrogate Championship show, held a few miles away from his home. A few hundred miles away, Hitler was marching on Poland – dog breeding had ceased to be one of the more important industries!" Only Daly could have called dog breeding an industry!

REGISTRATIONS

Kennel Club registrations for the new Boxer breed in those very early years are difficult to find. In 1938, I see from 'Boxer Broadcasts', the Boxer Breed notes in *Our Dogs*, contributed by Mr R.H.Voss of Bulldog fame, that 1938 finished with a total of 83 Boxer registrations, and for the next year, 1939, there were just 74 Boxers registered. Perhaps the war which broke out in September 1939 had an adverse effect. After all, the Boxer was not a small dog and at the beginning of the war there were rumours that there would be difficulties with feeding dogs in wartime. Registrations for Boxers at the Kennel Club tell the story of the wartime restrictions and the subsequent revival of the breed's fortunes.

1940: 33
1941: 31
1942: 9
1943: 139
1944: 246
1945: 399
1946: 707
1947: 412
1948: 1922
1949: 2644
1950: 3647
1951: 4464
1952: 4476
1953: 5592

By the 1950s the Boxer was fourth in the Kennel Club League table – a remarkable achievement for a breed that numbered only half a dozen, twenty years previously. Unfortunately, this massive Boxer population explosion was not for the good for the breed. People leapt on to the bandwagon, breeding indiscriminately. Some of the Boxers, sold as pet puppies, were inclined to be shelly and lacking in bone. There was a definite deterioration in temperament, many were shy and nervous, cringing away from strangers. I remember at this time, there was a trend towards 'miniature' Boxers – tiny creatures, about a foot high were being boasted about – thank goodness, nothing came of them! Serious breeders were more sensible, and they valued the Boxer breed too much to let this sort of thing catch on.

Chapter Four

THE BOXER DURING WORLD WAR II

WAR WORK

The war brought a new phase into Boxer life – war work! Guard dogs were needed all over the country, and at least three official organisations were actively recruiting dogs for this type of war work. Large dogs were in demand, and although the Boxer was a relatively new breed, they were among the dogs listed as suitable for guard work. Maybe the success of the German War Dog Brigade in the First World War had filtered through to Britain. Aerodromes and airfields, naval dockyards, army depots, prisoner of war camps, factories and workshops where tanks and ammunition were being made, were all places which had to be guarded. It was estimated that one well-trained guard dog could, in some cases, release one or even two soldiers for active war service. Quite a few Boxers were offered by their owners, and they joined the many dogs who had been recruited for this type of work.

In 1942 the War Office appealed in the press for dogs. Major Baldwin, who had for many years bred and exhibited the 'Picardy' Alsatians, was put in charge of the RAF Training School for Dogs in Cheltenham, and Mr H.S. Lloyd of the famous 'Ware' Cockers was involved in training dogs for the Army War Dogs Unit – both eminent and well-known dog men. Mrs M.E.O'Brien and her police dog trainer, Mr Sly, were recruiting dogs for the Ministry of Supply to guard factories, ammunition sites and depots.

The Boxer breeders, Miss Sinclair and Miss Clay, both sent Boxers to join Major Baldwin's RAF guard dogs. Friston Truda, known as 'Folly' left Millicent Sinclair's Boxer kennel in Ireland to go to Cheltenham, and she was much appreciated by Major Baldwin, who wrote that she was well, had settled down happily and he thought she would be very suitable for their work. Unfortunately, Millicent tells me that after the war when Folly returned home, she was never quite the same as when she went to war, and found it difficult getting back to family life. Miss Clay sent Kaspar of Fieldburcote, known as 'Kappy', who was also to become an RAF police

Friston Truda, known as Folly, was recruited for war work, and proved to be very successful carrying out her duties.

patrol dog. Sadly, he did not survive the return journey to Hertfordshire when he was crated, which was a sad way to end his war career.

There were many articles in the press and the dog papers about the training schools, describing the feeding, training and the luxury type of kennelling used for these war dogs. At one time, members of the ATS joined the schools to look after the dogs. The girls, who had been involved with dogs or worked in kennels, pre-war, were excellent kennel maids, and the dogs and the ATS were very happy with this move. Some dogs actually enjoyed army life, and strayed to army camps, or to airfields, apparently liking the hustle and bustle, the company, and the food. They were sometimes found safe and well by their frantic owners after several weeks or months of camp life!

Later, when the Americans joined the war, dogs in the USA were used to raise funds for the Red Cross and War Bonds, and some were later trained as guard dogs for large airfields. There was one Boxer, called 'Max', who got a lot of publicity for the breed because he loved jumping out of aeroplanes with the parachutists. He joined Fort Bennings Georgia Paratrooper Unit, and was awarded his Wings after five jumps with his unit! In 1944 there was a demonstration by the American Coast Guard Team and sentry dogs at Westminster show in New York. One of the team, a Boxer, clowning and, typically, playing to the audience, brought the house down and stopped the show. So Boxers were involved with the war on both sides of the Atlantic.

Kaspar of Fieldburcote, known as Kappy, served his country with honour from 1939 to 1945. Shown at Crufts in 1939.

The certificate awarded to Kappy for his loyal and faithful service.

THE FIGHTING FANCIER

Lance Corporal George Jakeman, of the 8th Army, had been a keen exhibitor and breeder of Greyhounds, Whippets, and Bulldogs in the Midlands for some years. In 1944 he wrote to Mr Voss of 'Boxer Broadcasts', *Our Dogs*, to say that he had a smashing young cropped Boxer dog puppy, red fawn, with a black mask, a white front and four white feet. Later it was heard that the 'Fighting Fancier', as MacDonald Daly called him, had shown a Boxer with some success at the Hamburg Show in 1945, and that he had "secured" from Frau Stockmann a brindle dog puppy called Collo von Dom, and that "he had played a part in breeding a litter in Germany, out of the famous Dutch Champion bitch, Favorite von Haus Germania".

Everyone who talks or writes about the 'Fighting Fancier' treads very cautiously and chooses their words with care, and, as far as I can see, there is still a bit of a mystery around his activities of that time. Some of the facts are that Ch. Favorite von Haus Germania was a beautiful bitch, made up before the war. She was owned and bred by Peter Zimmermann, one of the top breeders and exhibitors of Boxers in Holland. She had disappeared from his kennel towards the end of the war, and the next thing we know is that she is whelping a litter in Germany, and George Jakeman is involved. This litter was by Rex von Hohenheuffen, a Ch. Lustig von Dom grandson. Favorite, and one of the puppies, later returned with George Jakeman to the UK. The puppy was owned by Miss Cameron Bing of London, and was later campaigned by Jakeman to become Ch. Holger von Germania – British Boxer Champion No. 5, officially bred by Peter Zimmermann, who was still listed as the owner of the dam.

Holger was an influence on British Boxers, because he was the sire of Ch. Orburn Kekeri, one of the first Boxers to go Best in Show at an All Breeds Championship Show. From surviving photographs, we can see that she was an absolutely beautiful bitch with lovely graceful lines, and, in my opinion, she could win top awards in the show ring today. She, in turn, was the dam of Ch. Winkinglight Viking, the grandmother of Winkinglight Justice, and so great-grandmother of another fabulous, world-beating bitch, Ch. Wardrobes Miss Mink. In fact, most of the world-famous Wardrobes Boxers are descended from Winkinglight stock, and are therefore closely bred to Favorite, the Dutch Champion bitch.

George Jakeman's exploits in Germany were not at an end, as he was later in the Army of Occupation, and I understand, again from Mr Voss's breed notes, that George caused a bit of a shock when he turned up at a new billet complete with eight Boxers and two ferrets –I wish I had been there to see his arrival! Before he left Germany and the armed forces, George was invited to judge Boxers at the Hamburg Show, obviously the first British Boxer fancier to have that honour. He also secured

Peter Zimmermann: The well-known Dutch breeder and international judge, with his Dutch Champion Favorite von Haus Germania. This bitch later ended up in the hands of George Jakeman, the 'fighting fancier'.

a deal with Herr Leo Heilbig, the noted German Boxer judge, to purchase Champus von der Ficherhut, a two-year-old dog, who had been very successful in the show ring, going Best of Breed at the Hamburg Show in 1946 over 68 Boxers. Champus had also qualified as a first-class Obedience Dog, which is no easy matter in Germany.

He came to the UK, and was later sold to the well-known English all-rounder judge, Tom Scott, who gave many exhibitions with Champus, which were much enjoyed by the ringside and gave the general public an idea of how a Boxer could be trained. He was also the sire of Ch. Florri of Breakstones, the first Champion to be made up by Miss Dunkles and Mrs Gamble, two charming and very successful ladies in the 1950s and 1960s – but formidable to a young novice like myself. Their lovely bitch, Ch. Fenella of Breakstones, won seven CCs, and for three years in succession was the CC winner at the British Boxer Club Championship Show.

Meanwhile, George Jakeman was demobbed and back home, with Favorite and Holger in quarantine. He later mated Favorite to his Collo von Dom, and these two made an impression on Boxers in Britain. A Collo/Favorite daughter was the CC winning Christine of Breakstones, who was the dam of the two Breakstones

Champions, Florizel and Fenella. It was, in fact, Miss Dunkles and Mrs Gamble who saw Favorite and, knowing Peter Zimmermann, they told him of a good, cropped Dutch bitch in England. When Zimmermann came over to judge the British Boxer Club Championship Show in 1949, he saw and recognised Favorite, and she returned with him to Holland. The Kennel Club were informed, and George Jakeman was reprimanded for taking a dog without permission, and he was banned from attending any dog shows in the UK for some time – although there were rumours that he did attend a show in drag!

Despite the adverse publicity, I think we should all be grateful to George for bringing such splendid Boxers to the UK, and for influencing the breed over here. There is, however, one thing I cannot forgive him for, and that is the affix he used for Holger – 'Von Germania' is so close to Zimmermann's 'von Haus Germania' that it should never have been accepted. I wonder how many mistakes there were in pedigrees in the 1950s and 1960s.

THE WAR YEARS IN GERMANY

In Germany, the war had a far-reaching effect on Boxers and their breeders. They were better organised at the start, and everything concerning dog keeping was taken over by the State Organisation. The State created a German Dog Affair Department. The Army High Command was in charge of this department, and the dog press was filled with orders from the authorities. Among these orders was one forbidding all large dog shows, although small ones were still allowed. Dogs were wanted for war work, so a regulation was passed that at least one parent of a mating had to have a medal for Obedience.

As soon as war was declared, all dog breeders were reviewed and only the Obedience trained dogs received cards for food. Others got nothing, and it was forbidden to breed from them. Approved puppies were bought by the State, but Frau Stockmann wrote that the authorities were very different in this war compared to the 1914 war; very few dogs were returned after being given to the Reich. The von Dom Boxers had to be trained, and they had to show their paces every now and again to the authorities. In some cases, precious dogs were chosen for war work and were not returned.

Once again Philip Stockmann was involved, and this time his son was also in the Army, and eventually made a prisoner of war. There were many air-raids to contend with, and there was the continuous worry about food for the dogs. Collecting food, with no transport available, worried Friederun all the time. Towards the very end of the war, Philip returned home having been a prisoner for four months, but after a few weeks he was imprisoned again.

It was interesting to see how the Boxers reacted to the different nationalities of the soldiers of the Army of Occupation. The Poles were chased away; the Russians were terrified of the dogs and were eventually chased away, whereas the Americans, who knew and loved Boxers, were accepted quite happily. Eventually, when hostilities ceased, only a grand-daughter of the original von Dom bred Boxers was left, and she was used to be the start of the modern von Dom line.

In August 1945 Philip Stockmann died, aged sixty-eight, following an operation in a prison hospital. The whole Boxer world mourned the death of one of the great authorities of the breed. He had kept and bred Boxers continuously for thirty-five years since 1910. Fortunately, many of Philip Stockmann's articles and writings have been preserved by the Munich Boxer Club, and translations of some of these are available to us, and we are extremely lucky that there is an English version of Frau Freiderun Stockmann's book, *My Life with Boxers*. For this translation, we are indebted to Wilson Wiley of the Wardrobes Boxers, who, when in Germany, was given a copy of the German version of the book, which had been compiled by a Boxer enthusiast, who wanted to record Freiderun's life story with the von Dom Boxers.

Wilson Wiley thought that an English translation would be interesting for us, so asked his friend, Fitch Daglish, if he would be willing to undertake it. Unfortunately Fitch Daglish died before completing this, and the final translation was finished by Dr Frankling and my friends Jo Bromley and Giselle Fairbrother. Although I am absolutely enchanted by the book and strongly recommend it to all those interested in Boxers, I do sometimes feel that we are at a disadvantage, and we should never forget it is only a translation of a verbal interview with Frau Stockmann.

CAMPAIGN FOR A NEW BOXER CLUB

In the UK, in the last years of the war, there was an increasing urgency about a Boxer Club. For several years, enthusiasts were campaigning in the dog press for an official Boxer Club. After all, one was started in Ireland in 1944, with Michael Fitzgerald as the first secretary, a post taken over later by Millicent Sinclair.

Boxer Clubs, or even meetings of Boxer people to discuss the breed, were suggested, to be held in London, the Midlands and the North of England. Whenever the Kennel Club was approached, enquirers were told that there was already a Boxer Dog Club in existence, and were referred to the Secretary, Mrs Caro. Other members of the dormant Boxer Dog Club, Mr Allon Dawson and Mr McClandish, who was the president of the club, all tried to fend off these enquiries.

When Mrs Elizabeth Somerfield judged the Boxer classes at a smallish Wembley Show, her first appearance as a judge of Boxers, she found that "there were several dogs and bitches which were not typical of the Breed", and she considered "that the sooner the British Boxer Dog Club can be started up again, the better, so that a Boxer Show can be held under a suitable pre-war Championship Show judge of the breed." Almost immediately after that, Mr McClandish wrote in the Boxer Breed Notes that "until the war ends, the Kennel Club do not recognise any new specialist Club. It may be that in time a second Boxer Club may be an advantage, but it would be wise to wait until the return of the class of show which have real influence on breeds before splitting the support given by breeders to a Club. The breed has a very short history in this country, and it might be that united we stand divided we fall. New brooms sweep clean, but it is as well to know what requires sweeping."

In the same paper, there is a short article:-

BOXER CLUB TO RENEW ACTIVITIES

At a meeting of the executive Committee of the British Boxer Dog Club it was decided that the time had come to resume activities. To this end the Secretary will be glad to hear from those who are interested in the breed and to have application forms for them to become members. The Club is already in correspondence as to the holding of a specialised show for Boxers, and if the application for membership warrants it, further efforts to hold a show will be made. The Secretary will be glad to send a copy of the Standard of the Breed to anyone who applies to the Secretary, Mrs Caro, Park Lane, London.

It seems that the British Boxer Dog Club Executive Committee was concerned that new Boxer Clubs might spring up and queer their pitch! Obviously the instructions of this oddly-worded notice were understood, because we read a few weeks later that entries for a first show, an Open Show, were coming in fast. The judge was to be Tom Scott, who had awarded CCs to Boxers at Richmond Championship Show in 1939. And there, at that show, second in the Puppy Bitch Class, was a puppy called Tirkane Tell Tale, who was the first Boxer I put my hands on! In 1948 Tell Tale padded across the floor of a dimly-lit drawing room in Calcutta, followed closely by twelve red and white puppies, the smallest of which was to be mine. Sherry, my first Boxer, was the mother of the first litter I bred, and the grandmother of the first Boxer I took into the show ring. This was Onstage Sterling Silver, still my best-loved Boxer, who, with his grandmother Sherry, is behind almost every Boxer I have ever bred, and was the start of my involvment with the breed.

One of the top kennels at this time was the established Stainburndorf Boxers, owned by Allon Dawson, who was very much to the fore in breeding with his imports – although following the war, eyes were now being turned towards America rather than Germany. The up-and-coming Boxer kennels included Panfield, owned and run by Mrs Somerfield, and the Maspound Boxers, an extension of Mrs Kittie Guthrie's Great Dane kennel. Mrs Guthrie also had some influence on the Boxer, as she contributed the Boxer breed notes to *Dog World*. It was through these breed notes that the campaign for a new Boxer Club grew at this time. She was very helpful to new Boxer enthusiasts, as each week she serialised extracts of the Boxer Standard, approved by the British Boxer Dog Club, way back in 1938.

There had been considerable controversy over the Standard in the late 1930s, and the Munich Club had been arguing amongst themselves since the 1890s. It was Mrs Gaertner and Mrs Palmedo of the 'se Sumbula' Boxers who bought a version of the 1910 Munich Standard from Austria to America. At roughly the same time Allon Dawson had his version of the Munich Standard translated in the UK. However, this was not accepted by the British Boxer Dog Club, and it was not until 1938, when Jack Wagner and Philip Stockmann produced their English translation in America, that this version was submitted to the English Kennel Club and approved. It was this Standard that Mrs Guthrie started to serialise after the war.

It is interesting to read that Mr Voss in 'Boxer Broadcasts' in *Our Dogs* devoted an entire week's contribution trying to prove the Boxers in Germany were no longer numerically the strongest. He concluded his notes with the statement: "The German Reich does not possess more than 46 per cent of the World's Boxer population ... there is plenty of good and reliable stock which can be obtained from countries other than Germany ... if and when the importation of Boxers into England once more becomes a practical policy."

44

Chapter Five

BOXER REVIVAL

THE FIRST POSTWAR CHAMPIONSHIP SHOW

The first year after the War – 1946 – the newly-revived British Boxer Dog Club applied to the Kennel Club for Championship Show Status. This was approved, and so the club were able to organise a Championship Show where Kennel Club Challenge Certificates would be awarded. The first Championship Show for Boxers was arranged for October 1946. The judge was to be Jack Wagner from America, who was an eminent expert on the breed and had worked on a translation of the Boxer Standard with Herr Philip Stockmann, the Boxer Chief Breed Warden of Germany, so it was felt that he, Mr Wagner, would be ideal to give an insight on the breed. The British Boxer Dog Club had also applied to the Kennel Club for a change of name, to be called The British Boxer Club, by which it is known to this day, the first Boxer Club in the United Kingdom.

The initial Championship Show was to take place as near to the centre of Britain as possible, and Coventry was chosen, as being accessible by train for everyone who was interested. At this show, Best in Show and the dog CC – the very first to be awarded to a Boxer at a specialist Breed Show – went to Monarchist of Maspound, bred and owned by Mrs Kitty Guthrie. Monarchist had British breeding in the first generation – Stainburndorf, Panfield and Fieldburcote – but the grandparents all went back to German breeding, mainly the von Dom Boxers. The bitch CC went to Panfield Serenade, who had similar type of breeding, with International Ch. Lustig von Dom and Stainburndorf Zulu as her grandparents, so there was also German breeding behind the Bitch CC winner. The same can be said for the two Reserve CCs winners. The dog Reserve CC went to a very young Holger von Germania, George Jakeman's protege, who had a German father and a Dutch mother. The bitch Reserve CC winner was Mayerling Whisp, once again with Stainburndorf breeding, Jaguar and Zulu, behind her.

I have the feeling that Mr Wagner was looking for quality and possible elegance rather than substance, if he could find it. Unfortunately, he did not write a report on the exhibits; but he wrote an article immediately after the judging, giving his impressions of the show and of our Boxers:

I was delighted to accept the invitation of the British Boxer Club to judge at the first Ch. show of the breed in England, and would like to say how much I enjoyed the courtesy of the officials and to express my appreciation of the sporting spirit of the exhibitors. I had heard that the Boxer had become very popular in this country so appreciated the opportunity to meet the people and see the dogs.

I knew that the dogs would progress in the English Fancy, because, if for nothing else, the temperament of the breed makes them one of the most popular of dogs. I realised before I came over that the limited number of dogs you had to breed from caused by the inability to import, and the limited number here at the beginning of the war, would create great difficulty in improving the stock. Unless you are fortunate enough to see quite a number of the great dogs, it is not easy to interpret the Boxer Standard and create the type of dog that the originators of the breed, and the real tried and true fanciers of long standing, have in mind.

AMERICAN MISTAKES

The mistakes we are making, and have made in the past, in America are a bit more pronounced here. The head which is very difficult to breed needs a lot of improvement. I would also like to see more balance and elegance. With over 100 dogs shown under me, I feel that only about half a dozen could be rated as excellent; while there were a good many average dogs there were also a good many poor ones.

My greatest disappointment was in the bulkiness I found almost throughout, wide fronts, heavy shoulders going back to quite light hindquarters. I was disappointed also in the many wide-skulled, short-muzzled animals. I found more unsoundness in front quarters than hindquarters. In my opinion, the winning dog, Monarchist of Maspound, was far ahead of most of the competitors in general type, balance and movement, and with this he had quite a bit of elegance, whilst the head chiselling left something to be desired; he did not show the thick skull, and the muzzle was in better balance than in most of the dogs. With a bit of age I think he will show just about the right substance for a top quality Boxer.

The winning bitch, Panfield Serenade, had lots of style and elegance and was sound. I would like to have had the head a bit more chiselled and a more alert expression. From the winning dog back, I found almost half a dozen dogs in close similarity of general quality. The reserve dog, Holger von Germania, about 11 months old, had great quality, and should he attain good size, I believe he will be a top specimen. This youngster has the possibilities of improving the breed in England. The reserve bitch, Stainburndorf Penelope, also excellent in basic qualifications with one exception, she has a tendency towards cow hocks, although she does not display any particular weakness in movement.

Among the other dogs that I thought were better than the average quality were the winning bitch puppy, Panfield Charlotte; the second bitch puppy, Dolores of Cremyll; the winning bitch in limit, Mayerling Whisp; 1st and 2nd in limit dogs, Gremlin Gunner and Stainburndorf Jaguar respectively, and 1st in open dogs, Irish Ch. Stainburndorf Bombard.

BRITISH BREEDERS HAVE DONE WELL
Under the conditions, I think the British breeders have done exceptionally well, and I hope to be back here again after there have been some good importations. I am sure today's breeders' enthusiasm and interest will mean tremendous improvement in a very short time.

We have been fortunate enough in the USA to have such famous imports as Int. Ch. Dorian von Marienhof, Utz von Dom, Lustig von Dom and Int. Ch. Sigurd von Dom to use as patterns and try to improve upon, and now we are fortunate enough to have the last famous Sieger, Int. Ch. Karlo v.d. Wolfsschlucht.

I feel that the English breeders have to some degree lost sight of the fact that the Boxer is fundamentally a working dog and such a dog must be able to jump a 6 to 8 ft fence, and must be able to travel at top speed for great distances. Such a dog cannot be found in the Mastiff and the Bulldog. He must be on the order of a powerful Terrier in the body build, with good length of leg, short, powerful back. In addition, as a companion and show dog, he should have the length of neck, head-chiselling and reasonably narrow skull that makes for great beauty in a dog.

Unfortunately, none of the Boxer CC winners from the five pre-war shows were still alive. The first-ever Boxer Champion, Horsa of Leith Hill, died during the war at only three and a half years of age; the bitches, Stainburndorf Wendy and Vanda and Gold of Uttershill, all died during the war when whelping or very soon after, although luckily, some of their progeny survived to be bred from.

Concentrating on the same kind of breeding as many of the winners of that first Championship Show, by the late 1940s we were getting a few of the type of Boxers which, even today, would be acceptable. The photographs of Ch. Orburn Kekeri and perhaps Ch. Bobby Sox of Greentubs, in the *BBC Record Book,* show much the same graceful, elegant type of Boxer.

ABOVE: Maspound Amos of Fieldburcote (ex Gold of Uttershill, CC winner in 1939). Grandfather of Ch. Alrakim Orburn Akaboo and her sister, Orburn Kekeri – a lovely bitch whose name appears in almost every pedigree of British-born Boxers.

Fall.

LEFT: Ch. Winkinglight Viking: He was one of the early English greats winning thirteen CCs – a record at that time. He was widely used at stud, siring five British Champions. He was born in 1948 and made up in 1950.

It is very interesting to see how involved George Jakeman was in the first couple of years of winning Boxers, firstly through Holger von Germania, and then through Bucko, Faust, and Lustig – the three Gardas Hoftsee litter brothers, bred by Mr Van den Bergh in Holland, at George's personal request. Undoubtedly, the bitch CC winner at that first Championship Show, Ch. Panfield Serenade, influenced British breeding in that decade, mostly due to the programme carried out by Mrs Dibby Somerfield (then Montgomery).

Ch. Panfield Serenade was already the result of a daughter/grandson mating. Alma von der Frankenwart, the Lustig von Dom daughter, was put to her grandson, Juniper of Bramblings. The same kind of mating for Alma was planned for the next year, when she was then mated to her kennel mate, Panfield Flack, whose breeding was totally German, and produced Panfield Tango. Two years later, Tango and Serenade were mated, producing Ch. Panfield Ringleader, arguably the Boxer sire of all time. To this day, many of our Boxers are descended from this great pre-potent Panfield stud dog. Looking at his pedigree, it is interesting to note just how many times International Champion Lustig von Dom features. Both in the United States and in the UK, the pre-potent Int. Ch. Lustig von Dom has had many fine descendants of which to be proud. Ch. Panfield Ringleader's children and grandchildren were still much in evidence in pedigrees right through to the end of the 1950s.

Another of those very early Champions to make a mark, was George Jakeman's Ch. Holger von Germania. Although Peter Zimmermann is credited with his breeding, Holger was the result of the Favorite litter bred by Jakeman in Germany at the end of the war. Holger was the sire of that beautiful bitch Ch. Orburn Kekeri, and her not-so-glamorous sister, Ch. Orburn Akaboo. Their mother had much the same breeding as Monarchist of Maspound, the first CC winner after the war. It was Ch. Orburn Kekeri, put to a Favorite half-brother, which founded the Winkinglight line of truly wonderful sires of Champions. This line had an influence on the Boxer breed until the late 1960s through those glamorous Wardrobes Boxers, bred by Mrs Connie Wiley. These Boxers had superb quality, probably inherited from the lovely Ch. Orburn Kekeri.

THE NORTH-SOUTH DIVIDE

When I first became involved in the show scene in the mid-1950s, there was a marked difference between the Boxers in the South and those in the North. The types were very different, and this was very obvious when you were travelling nationwide to attend different shows. Although Britain is a small country, at that time communications were difficult, and the inability to move easily around the UK influenced the type of the Boxer. The Northern Boxer Club was formed by Allon Dawson as soon as he left the committee of the British Boxer Club. He became chairman, with Philip Dyson as secretary. Mr Dawson was very insistent that the new club should follow his own translation of the Munich Boxer Standard, and so for many years there were two Standards being followed by the two Boxer Clubs. The Boxers in the North had great substance and nobility. They had very beautiful heads with strong muzzles. They were shown on loose leads, standing up and looking superb. The main faults were that these Boxers did not have good toplines, backs were inclined to roach, and they did fall off in croup.

In the South, Boxers had more elegance, they were of lighter build, and the heads were inclined to lack muzzle, and were longer. In many cases, these dogs were overhandled, almost to the extent that they were topped and tailed. The difference in these two types could be seen immediately. I can remember getting out of the car at the Corn Exchange, Leeds, where the show was taking place, and being completely overcome by the look of the heads, the expressions and the presence of the Northern Boxers!

In the North, there was the Stainburndorf Boxer kennel, Philip and Evelyn Dyson's Oidar (Radio backwards!), later Knowle Crest Boxers, who were a great influence, while in the South, the American imports, Mazalaine Texas Ranger, Ch. Awldogg Southdowns Rector, and Flip of Belorina were much-used and were the main influence. It was only when the Midland Boxer Club was formed, and with the emergence of the Winkinglight Boxers, that the two types began to merge together. Certainly, when the Winkinglight dogs became a well-used stud force, the type of our Boxers began to level out – I suspect that the increase of the motorway system had something to do with it.

Chapter Six

INFLUENTIAL KENNELS

REGISTRATIONS

In 1951, the number of Boxers registered at the Kennel Club reached 4,500, having increased very rapidly, by about 1,000 per year, since the 400 which were registered in the last year of the war. During the next ten years, up to 1960, 113 Champions were made up. Some forty years later, we have about 500 Champions!

The two British Boxer Club Record Books, Volumes I and II, contain photographs, details and a full pedigree of every Boxer who has been made into a Champion to the present day. The first Volume of the Record Book contains details collected by Mrs Somerfield for her own interest. She wrote to every owner and asked them to send a photograph and pedigree of their new Champion as it was made up. Volume II, which has extended pedigrees (five generations), has given the compilers, Linda Carnaby and Robert MacDougal, many sleepless nights! However, these two books are an invaluable source of reference.

By 1970, 230 Boxer Champions had been made up. The Kennel Club registrations for the breed had climbed to over 7,000, but since then have levelled off to about 6,000 a year. Each year, the Kennel Club allocate to every breed a number of Challenge Certificates to be awarded at Championship Shows, and this number depends on the number of registrations of that breed. The Boxer, still being in the top ten of the breed popularity poll, is allocated about thirty sets of CCs a year

It is an impossible task to attempt to detail all the successful show dogs over the last forty years, and so I am highlighting the more important kennels and the dogs who have influenced our present-day Boxers.

In the Boxer breed, there have been some very large establishments, both for breeding and showing, such as the Stainburndorf kennel in Yorkshire, the Burstall kennel near Ipswich, and the Summerdale Boxers and Great Dane kennel at Liss in Hampshire. These three establishments, owned by Allon Dawson, Major Douglas Bostock and Martin Summers respectively, were probably a progression from the packs of hounds or shooting dogs kept by the landed gentry. People who had always had an interest in dogs brought new and imported breeds, such as the Boxer, into their kennels – and in those days there were legal tax rebates. These three establishments were run as a business on large country estates. Dogs were bought in because they were already Champions, because they had already won well at shows and so might be made up, or because of their breeding potential.

The matings were often decided by the kennel managers, and puppies were picked out of the nest by the kennel managers and trained for the show ring by the kennel manager or his staff. These managers probably knew dogs and possibly had some experience in a breed, and with any luck, that breed might have been Boxers! There might have been some discussion with the owner as to the matings and possibly where to show a particular dog, but the dogs were taken to the shows and handled by the kennel managers. This attitude of treating dogs as a business altered Boxer breeding and showing, I feel, to a disadvantage. Certainly, those of us with just a couple of dogs with which to compete, were absolutely out-gunned, and were far from happy about it.

STAINBURNDORF

Based in Otley, Yorkshire, Allon Dawson's many early Continental imports were invaluable, as were his contacts in Germany, and we, in Boxers, should always be extremely grateful to him. The Stainburndorf kennel was run by Arthur Round, the kennel manager, who was a dog man of the old school, always neat and tidy in his uniform of brown kennel overalls. Actually, I am sure that Allon Dawson made the decisions as to the matings of his dogs, but the rest was left to Arthur Round and his kennel staff. This would have included the whelpings, probably the choice of pups, and certainly weaning, feeding and some show training. Mr Round was well-known for appearing in the ring in his overalls, and standing immobile, with a Boxer at the end of a long lead. He certainly knew all about the development of Boxer puppies, and was highly respected by many Boxer breeders.

I well remember Mrs Cooke (Greentubs) and I having a conversation with him at the Leeds Show, when he told us that you should always give a puppy time to "come together". This was said with a great deal of expressive hand movement. We were so amused by his description, and for many years after that we waited for our puppies to "come together!"

When Allon Dawson died in 1960, the kennel was wound up, and the Stainburndorf affix was left to Peggy Penn, who lived quite near, in Yorkshire, and who had used many of the Stainburndorf dogs at stud, and founded her Boxers on Stainburndorf stock. Peggy went on showing and breeding, and she made up a number of her own 'new' Stainburndorf Champions. On one occasion, I drove up to Otley and met Allon Dawson, and I used several of the Stainburndorf stud dogs – several, because at that time Arthur Round was in hospital. The dogs were in charge of the gardeners, who were acting as kennel staff, and the dogs had put on weight. With the help of the gardener, who held the dogs, and the gardener's boy, who kept up a running commentary, all came to a miserable end, with several fat Boxers puffing and blowing, and totally exhausted. Nine weeks later my bitch had seven puppies, but as I had no idea which of the dogs was the sire, I did not feel able to keep any of the puppies as I was unsure of the breeding! After this abortive trip I now know there is no need for a 'mating'.

The final tally for the Stainburndorf kennel was sixty CC winners, and seven Champions.

BURSTALL

It was in those early days that Major Bostock followed Allon Dawson's example, and he established his Burstall Boxer kennel, near Ipswich in Suffolk. Major Bostock was well-known in the animal world, through the Bostock Circus and Menagerie, and he brought his expert knowledge of breeding and animal welfare to the Burstall Boxer kennel. He started with some home-bred dogs, and he bought in Dutch and German stock. Imports also came from America; they were mainly Champions, and well-bred brood bitches. He was lucky to have advice from Andrew Thomson, who was in the area after war service.

Beaulaines Bonadea: A daughter of the great Am. Ch. Bangaway of Sirrah Crest. Dam of Ch. Burstall Fireaway and Ch. Burstall Zipaway.

Peggy Green, later Peggy Thomson, was Major Bostock's kennel manager, and Beryl Alderton was on her kennel staff. (I mention these two names as they feature in the *BBC Record Book* as breeders or owners of Champion Boxers.) There were many excellent Boxers in the Burstall kennel; many of them were bought in as promising prospects, or had already been made up, but quite a few good dogs were bred at the kennel. Significant imports were also made from America, including Beaulaines Bonadea, a daughter of the great Am. Ch. Bangaway of Sirrah Crest, who was imported in whelp to Ch. Mazalaine Gallantry. She whelped her litter in quarantine, and two of the pups were made up, Ch. Burstall Fireaway and Ch. Burstall Jazzaway. These two dogs, with that excellent American breeding, were used a great deal at stud and so influenced our Boxers. Another of the Burstall American imports was Rob Roy of Tomira, and his grandson, Ch. Burstall Clarion Call, who was one of my very favourites – a short coupled, neat dog, who had great presence. The Burstall stud dogs sired a total of thirty-five CC winners, which accounted for six Champions. It is interesting to note that Bonadea produced seven CC winners and two Champions, which is a good number for a bitch.

In this type of establishment, money and distance of travel was no object when campaigning a number of dogs and bitches at the same time. They were taken to shows and handled by the kennel manager. This method of dog breeding and showing was a cross between the American method of putting a dog out to a handler for the show season, and having a race horse in training over here! Peggy Thomson was married at that time to Andrew Thomson, who was one of the early pioneers in Boxers. Peggy, an expert handler, was able to get the best out of all the dogs, and the dogs were certainly devoted to her. This was certainly reflected in the number of CCs awarded.

Previously, breeders had been content to win three CCs so that the dog was a Champion, and leave it at that. Now things changed. Panfield Ringleader won eight CCs, Winkinglight Viking won thirteen, and Burstall Delight notched up eleven, and so a kind of race began. Peggy Thomson's lovely bitch Geronimo Carissima amassed seventeen CCs, which remained a record for a bitch for some time – overtaken only by Ch. Seefeld Picasso and Ch. Gremlin Inkling, each winning twenty-four CCs. After that, the outstanding Ch. Marbelton Desperate Dan went to the top with twenty-nine CCs, topped in 1977 by Ch. Gremlin Summer Storm with thirty-three CCs. His breeding, incidentally, went straight back to Gremlin Inkspot, Marian Fairbrother's first Champion, born in 1949.

Major Bostock was, for many years, the chairman of the British Boxer Club and later president of the club. After his death and the dispersal of the Burstall kennel, Peggy, now Peggy Haslam, joined the Summerdale Boxer and Great Dane kennels.

Marion Fairbrother ran the Boxer kennel in partnership with Martin Summers, while Peggy Haslam was in charge of the Danes. Alan, Peggy's husband, started to handle professionally for other people and was quite successful – the first professional Boxer handler in the UK.

SUMMERDALE

The Summerdale Boxer and Great Dane kennels were at Martin Summers' estate at Upham House, a lovely Tudor mansion at Liss in Hampshire. Martin Summers and Marion Fairbrother formed a partnership in both Danes and Boxers, and they decided to base the Boxer breeding on American stock. Marion went to the USA, where she found two excellent Boxers to import, Rainey Lane Sirrocco and Rainey Lane Milltown. It was thought, rather unkindly, that Milltown was sent over as a companion to Sirrocco. However, these two dogs were the foundation stock for the Summerdale Boxer kennel.

Sirrocco was particularly successful, siring sixty-seven CC winners and Reserve CC winners. A dozen of these were Summerdale dogs and bitches; the rest belonged to a number of different breeders, and Summerdale and Gremlin Boxers feature behind many of our present-day dogs. I associate the Boxers of the Summerdale era with bright fawn-and-white, compact Boxers, such as Shatter, Shamus, Snazzy, Southpaw and Defender, and, very typical of this kennel, Summerdale Logic.

During the partnership at Summerdale, most of the litters bred at Upham, those lovely reds, carried the Summerdale affix, but there were some brindles, such as Ch. Summerdale Normlin Freelancer, Ch. Gremlin Normlin Legend and Ch. Gremlin Normlin Notanda, bred by friends of Marion, Norman and Linda Archer, but they seemed to be a different type, more rangy, and they did not appeal to me so much.

Martin Summers was extremely generous to us all as he entertained us at Upham House for the British Boxer Club Championship Shows for several years, giving us marvellous lunches, in pink-and-white striped marquees, and he is still a vice-president of the Club.

GREMLIN

When Martin Summers had to give up the kennel, Marion Fairbrother revived her Gremlin line of Boxers. The late 1950s can truly be called the Ch. Gremlin Inkling era. Inkling was a tall, upstanding fawn and white dog, with a very pleasing head and beautiful expression. I saw and admired him many times.

I remember, with pleasure, Gremlin Mere Magic, who, I think, was unlucky not to gain her title. However, she has been a great influence on the breed as she was the dam of one of the best of the Gremlins, a top winner, Gremlin Summer Storm, who won thirty-three CCs – a record in the breed for a very long time. Ch. Gremlin Summer Storm sired many top winners, including seven Champions and eight Reserve CC winners, including Ch. Summerdale Summer Shadow of Gremlin, who was the last of the Gremlin Boxers made up in 1983, ending a line which boasted 170 CC winners and a dozen Champions. It is quite amazing that one kennel can span so many years successfully.

PANFIELD
Run by Dibby Somerfield, this was a highly efficient kennel dating from the early days of Boxers until the late 1970s when the last of her homebred Panfield Champions, Gold Bangle, was made up. Following Dibby's death, Stafford Somerfield has kept the Panfield flag flying.

Two Champions from the early 1950s: Ch. Toplocks Welladay of Sheafdon (left) and her son, Ch. Sheafdon Spellmaker, sired by the well-known American import, Mazelaine's Texas Ranger.

Dibby planned the matings, whelped and reared the puppies, and chose the ones to keep, show-trained the pups herself, and handled them in the ring. The dogs were always well turned out, and impeccably show-trained. They were always handled on a loose lead – very seldom was a hand put on them, and they were trained to move impeccably, just at the right speed, and always turned at the end of the ring in a circle – the dog never stopping in its stride – to come back to the judge. It was really a joy to behold. 'Topping and tailing', the American style of handling, came in some time later, but it was unheard of in the early days.

A beautifully-bred dark brindle and white Boxer dog, called Mazelaine's Texas Ranger, was imported from America. He was a gift to Dibby Somerfield from Mr and Mrs Wagner of the famous Mazelaine kennels in Texas. 'Tex' was an extremely good Boxer with a charming character, and he proved to be an outstanding sire. Among his many top winners was Ch. Panfield Texas Tycoon, winner of eight CCs and twenty Reserve CCs. He was a particular favourite of mine – such a charming dog; a good showman, very striking, and well-made throughout.

Through the great, and beautifully line-bred, Ch. Panfield Ringleader, the first pre-potent stud dog who sired seven Champions and winners of forty CCs, and the imported Mazelaine Texas Ranger, whose sons and daughters won thirty-three CCs between them, six becoming Champion, this kennel had an enormous influence on the breed. All of us in the breed should be eternally grateful to Dibby Somerfield for her intuitive line breeding of Ringleader in the very early days, and for the encouragement and advice she gave to us very willingly. The final tally for this kennel was about 200 CC winners.

WARDROBES

The Wardrobes kennel in Princes Risborough, Buckinghamshire, was successful from the 1950s to the 1970s, and was run by Connie Wiley, aided and abetted by her solicitor husband, Wilson. Connie had been at the top for many years in the horse business, both as a breeder and as an exhibitor. Her Boxers were always turned out superbly, and they were impeccably presented in the show ring by Connie herself. Some of the most beautiful Boxers I have ever seen were from Wardrobes.

The Wardrobes Boxer kennels was extremely professional, and Connie took care of all planning. She decided which dogs to use at stud, whelped the litters, chose the puppies from the nest, decided which shows to attend, and which dogs to take. She trained all the dogs for the show ring, and very often sat with the youngsters on the bench until they were used to dog shows. The Wardrobes kennel remained at the top of the breed and was respected worldwide for well over twenty years. The kennel's first Champion was Ch. Wardrobes Alma of Grenovia, a Ringleader daughter, born

Connie Wiley of the Wardrobes Boxers, judging the Scottish Boxer Club Championship Show in 1959. The dog CC winner (left) is Ch. Wynskip Crofter and the bitch CC winner is Ch. Wild Star of Greentubs, handled by Mrs Cooke.

in 1950, and made up the next year, and the last big win came in 1973 when Ch. Claire de Lune won her thirty-first CC.

Wardrobes Miss Mink is the most memorable of the Wardrobes Boxers. The reason I think she was outstanding was her outlook and general behaviour. I never saw her ruffled, everything was taken in her stride. She had been very well and sympathetically show trained. She always stood four-square, perfectly still, with her neck arched, surveying everything that was going on around her. When she moved, she flowed along. I do not think I ever saw her have a cross word with any other Boxer in the ring, in fact other dogs were just looked upon as necessary extras. Mink was a dark red with very little white markings. She had a good black mask, with no white at all on her head. Her eyes were dark, and so bright that the look seemed to glow. In fact, she was as near to perfection as I have ever seen. I feel that we shall not see the likes of Miss Mink again, and I doubt if we shall ever see a Boxer with that assured ring presence again.

After the fabulous Miss Mink, whom I adored and remember playing with in one of the barns at Wardrobes, my favourite was her son, Wild Mink. He always stood four square in the ring, at the end of a long lead, very calmly surveying the scene around him, beautifully handled by his breeder, Connie Wiley.

MASPOUND

Another large kennel establishment in the pioneering Boxer days was the Maspound kennel of Boxers and Danes, owned and run by Mrs Kitty Guthrie. I saw Mrs Guthrie judging a Boxer Championship Show in 1959. It was a lovely sunny day at Cheltenham, and I was very impressed with her very deliberate manner and decisive judging. Her dog, Mitsuko of Maspound, was a very smart red and white and put on an excellent performance in the ring, but unfortunately it was found that he was unable to sire puppies, so there were never any Mitsuko sons and daughters to carry on, and the Maspound Boxers died out.

FELCIGN

The Felcign Boxers were bred and exhibited by one of the outstanding characters of the breed. Felicia Price was such an ebullient character that it is impossible to think of her dogs without writing about Felicia herself. One of the first Felcign stud dogs

The Southern Counties Championship Show, 1960. The bitch CC winner (left) is Ch. Wardrobes Silhouette of Arnogor, handled by Connie Wiley, and the dog CC winner is Ch. Felcign Hot Cargo, handled by Felicia Price. The judge is Jean Haggie of the Sheafdon Boxers..

was Faro, bought from Jean Haggie in a 'job lot' of puppies to sell on. Felicia saw the potential in Faro, who eventually sired four Champions, who in turn collected a total of eighteen CCs. I always think of the Felcign Boxers as being very smart, red and white, with exceptional toplines and tail-sets. The Felcign kennels eventually amassed nearly eighty CCs between fourteen Champions. The great Makreen Tam O'Shanter, bred by Felicia's friend, Dr McKellar, was absolutely beautiful. She was sired by Felcign Hot Diggotty.

WITHERFORD
The Witherford Boxers were also started in the 1950s when Mrs Pat Withers was in partnership with George Jakeman, and Pat has been most successful with her Boxers. Five Witherford stud dogs were made up, and Ch. Witherford Cool Mango sired seven Champions, three for other kennels. The Witherford stud dogs were responsible for their stock winning 120 CCs; nineteen English Champions were made up, nine of these were for other kennels.

However, Pat Withers' main success has been on the Continent with Witherford Satan's Touch and, more recently, Ch. Witherford Hot Chestnut. Hot Chestnut has earned the titles of International Champion, World Champion, German Bundesseiger and Klubseiger, and has been used at stud all over the Continent, having been imported by Karen Rezewski in Bremen. So the Witherford dogs (mostly named after colours of nail varnish) have spread their style and breeding far and wide. An import of Pat Withers was Xanti von Dom, brought over after a visit to Frau Stockmann in the 1960s, and later taken to America by Maud Payton Smith.

WINKINGLIGHT
The Winkinglight Boxer kennel, owned by Mrs Hullock, was, like Witherford, based in the Midlands. Viking and Justice were produced here, the latter being the sire of many of the Wardrobes Boxers. Winkinglight Jandan Jupiter was responsible for two of the Witherford Champions – Crystal Clear and Sweet Talk – and also Witherford's Satan's Touch. The Winkinglight dogs sired fifteen Champions and their children won 90 CCs.

OIDAR/KNOWLE CREST
The North of England was represented by Philip and Evelyn Dyson, who started early on with some Stainburndorf Zulu stock. Their affix started off as Oidar (radio backwards) as Philip owned a wireless shop. Later, Philip and Evelyn changed their affix to the more up-market Knowle Crest. The homebred Meteor of Knowle Crest was a lovely dog. They had six good bitches – three were Champions – and they

produced successful show-winning stock, with twenty-six CCs and five Champions between them.

SEEFELD

This was a very successful kennel in the South West, making up fifteen Champions, and the Seefeld-bred stock won nearly 300 CCs between them, and are still winning! My very favourite was Ch. Seefeld Art Master, who sired five Champions, but this figure was easily surpassed by his father, Picasso, who sired eighteen Champions.

Pat Heath has judged at Championship show level all over the world, and Seefeld Boxers have won and become Champions in many countries. Sheila Bowman has joined the Seefeld Boxers, and several American dogs have been imported by this kennel.

Ch. Seefeld Picasso: Winner of 24 CCs, his offspring went on to win 105 CCs and 93 Reserve CCs. Bred by Pat Heath.

A line-up of seven Champions, all daughters of Ch. Seefeld Picasso. Pictured left to right: Ch. Lester Lucky Lady, Ch. Seefeld Coral Dawn, Ch. Calidad Bright Boots, Ch. Kinvike Kollectors Item, Ch. Coperscope Wynbok Sophia, Ch. Faerdorn Truly Gorgeous and Ch. Steymere Ritzi Miss.

WINUWUK

This kennel, owned by Ivor and Marion Ward Davies, is also based in the South West. They were great admirers of American Boxers, so they imported a great sire, Kreyond Back in Town of Winuwuk. He was widely used, and has been a great influence, passing on his beautiful head and expression, which seems to last for many generations. Back in Town sired four Champions, and his offspring were winners of twenty-four CCs.

Their other American import was Winuwuk Milrays Red Baron of Valvays, who was also a good sire responsible for three Champions and for stock winning forty-five CCs. The kennel had three Champions, including Good Golly, winner of twenty-five CCs. She was a particularly good bitch, with a lovely outline, and I am pleased to say that I awarded her a Reserve CC. The Winuwuk stock was responsible for winning 114 CCs and they are still winning today with a new young team to handle their dogs.

SKELDER

The Skelder Boxers are owned by Joy Malcolm, whom I always envy as she used Frohlich von Dom back in the distant past! Since those days, Joy has built up a very successful kennel based on a very good bitch line. Stud dogs from all kennels are used, but only after their stock has been seen, and I feel that Joy Malcolm is one of the really clever breeders.

Eight Skelder Champions have been made up, and Skelder bitches have amassed over seventy CCs. The dogs have been responsible for thirty CCs, which speaks volumes for the Skelder bitch line. I gave a CC to Burnt Almond, who was a lovely bitch, and Burnt Offering was named after my cooking!

BILORAN

Bill and Ann Law are the owners of the Biloran Boxer kennel, and all their dogs are named after characters from the novels of Charles Dickens. They have bred some excellent Boxers, and I have given CCs to two of them. They were Mr Similarity, a wonderful dog of great substance and style, and show presence, who is my idea of a really good Boxer, and Miss Nancy (sired by Mr Similarity), who was a great show girl, extremely well made, with a beautiful head and a charming expression. The Biloran Boxers have won many CCs.

TYEGARTH

Blue Kiwi was bred by Sheila Cartwright, the owner of the Tyegarth affix, which is also well-known for its Champion Bulldogs. The Tyegarth top stud dogs were her

Biloran Cherry Pecksniff: A fine example of the Biloran Boxers, owned by Anne and Bill Law.

Pearce.

own Ch. Famous Grouse, Ch. Tyegarth Glenmorangie of Jenroy, owned and made up by Mrs Jenny Townsend, and Ch. Tyegarth Blue Kiwi, owned and made up by Vince and Annabelle Zammit. Between them, these three dogs have sired some thirty Champions (with Grouse being responsible for seventeen Champion sons and daughters) and have sired stock who have won a total of almost 200 CCs, coming close to the Wardrobes record of CCs.

When Ch. Tyegarth Famous Grouse started producing very good quality Boxers, he began to be used, quite rightly, by many current Boxer breeders. The Faerdorn,

Ch. Tyegarth Famous Grouse: Winner of 11 CCs and 11 Reserve CCs. His offspring won at least 129 CCs and 117 Reserve CCs.

A good British head: Ch. Tyegarth Pink Pussycat (The Jacobite of Tyegarth – Tyegarth Parfait Amour).

Banks.

Sheffordian, Blupines, Carinya, Sunhawk/Norwatch and the Glenfall kennels all used Grouse with a great deal of success, so that many breeding lines have been improved by the great Grouse.

SUNHAWK/NORWATCH
The Sunhawk/Norwatch Boxers are owned by Helen and Eddie Banks, and they have enjoyed a good deal of success. Helen's Norwatch Mustang Wine is certainly a marvellous producer, with a tally of three Champion sons and two Champion daughters. Mustang Wine features three times in the pedigree of the present top Boxer in the country, Ch. Tonatron Glory Lass. Another of Mustang Wine's Champion progeny, Ch. Norwatch Brock Buster, was also a great producer, siring three Champions and five top winners, including Sheffordian Ruby Tuesday of Norwatch to whom I gave the Reserve CC at Crufts. Mustang Wine's children won a total of fifty-seven CCs, with Brockbuster gaining twenty-nine CCs.

Ch. Norwatch Brockbuster: Winner of 29 CCs and 22 Reserve CCs including BOB at Crufts 1983. His offspring have won 21 CCs and 21 Reserve CCs.

P. Holley.

RAYFOS

Norwatch Mustang Wine also produced Ch. Norwatch Glory Boy of Rayfos for Philip and Barbara Greenway. The Greenways bought their first Boxer, Sheafdon Medalist, from Jean Haggie as a 21st birthday present for Philip. Medalist's son, Rayfos Rainmaker, was my first ever CC winner. Rayfos Cockrobin, and his father, Norwatch Glory Boy of Rayfos, between them produced five Champions and were responsible for forty-six CCs. Cockrobin, my top winner at Crufts, is the grandfather of Ch. Sulez Whatever you say ('Boss'), who is featured on the jacket of this book.

TONANTRON

Norwatch Glory Boy of Rayfos is also the great-grandfather of today's top Boxer, appearing three times in the pedigree of Ch. Tonantron Glory Lass, who holds the record with forty-four CC to date. She is the result of several generations of Boxer breeding for Mr and Mrs Tonkin, who have used many good Boxer Champions, including Steynmere Night Rider, Ackendene Willy Wagtail and Tyegarth Famous Grouse. They then made up Tonantron Glory Girl; her father, Tonantron True Glory,

Ch. Tonantron Glory Lass: Breed record holder with a tally of 44 CCs. She is pictured with her owner and breeder Sagra Tonkin and the British Boxer Club Champion of Champions trophy, won again in August 1993.

when mated to a Tonantron bitch produced the glorious Glory Lass. Living in faraway Cornwall one cannot but admire them for the long distances they have had to travel in order to win the record number of CCs and Reserve CCs.

ACKENDENE

This kennel is owned and run by June Grover, who started breeding Boxers in the 1950s. Her first Champion was Ch. Ackendene Royal Fern, who was made up in 1966, but my favourite was Ch. Ackendene Royal St John (called after the famous footballer). 'Scroggie', as he was known to his friends, won nine CCs, and was also used at stud.

June has also had some very nice bitches who won CCs, especially Ch. Ackendene Precious Bane, a grand-daughter of Royal Fern, who won eight CCs.

More recently, Ch. Ackendene Willy Wagtail and Ch. Ackendene Royal Streaker of Zondora have enjoyed success in the show ring with a combined tally of sixteen CCs. Willy Wagtail was the father of Ch. Antrom Prize Guy, the first Champion made up by Mr and Mrs Tonkin, who later changed their affix to Tonantron and hit the highspots with Ch. Tonantron Glory Lass. June has recently imported stud dogs from America, including an American Champion.

FAERDORN

I am sure that Miss Susan Harvey will not mind me saying that, like me, she goes back a long way in the Boxer world. She was involved with the Wardrobes and Panfield kennels some years ago, and was a great friend of Dibby Somerfield. Her first Champion, Faerdorn Truly Scrumptious was made up in 1970 and on Dibby's advice, she was mated to the great Ch. Seefeld Picasso, and produced Ch. Faerdorn Truly Gorgeous. These two bitches were excellent and so typey.

Ch. Faerdorn Pheasant Plucker: Winner of 24 CCs and 10 Reserve CCs. His offspring have won 39 CCs and 34 Reserve CCs. Daniel, was a very good mover.

Truly Gorgeous was the dam of Gold Bangle of Panfield, the last Boxer Dibby Somerfield made up before her death, and the grandmother of Sue Harvey's top stud dog, Ch. Faerdorn Pheasant Plucker. He was the sire of eight good Champions, seven of these for other kennels, and his sons and daughters were responsible for thirty-nine CCs. Most notable of his progeny are Ch. Faerdorn Flash Bang Wollop, winner of six CCs, and Bitza Shout And Roar, now owned by Mr and Mrs Varney, who has won fifteen CCs to date. This speaks well for Faerdorn breeding.

MARBELTON
The highly successful Marbelton Boxer kennel is run and owned by John and Mary Hambleton, and the dogs are campaigned by Mary. Since making up Ch. Marbelton Top Mark, their first Champion, they have gone from strength to strength. Top Mark sired three Champion dogs and two Champion bitches. His top winner, and my very favourite, was Int. Ch. Marbelton Desperate Dan, who won twenty-nine CCs, and then produced three Champions himself. Dan was really an outstanding Boxer, oozing charisma, and a good showman. I first judged him on his second birthday, and Mary said I had spoilt his birthday by only giving him a third prize! Luckily she, being a good sport, brought him to me again, and this time, at the LKA, I awarded

Annabel and Vince Zammit's Ch. Satonoaks Robbie Redcoat: Sire of two Champions; he has produced 11 different Green Card winners to date.

him his twenty-fifth CC. Mary and John's kennel suffered under the blight of Progressive Axonpathy, and they imported dogs from the Continent to enable them to resurrect their kennel. Having made up eleven Champions before the black PA days, their new stud force have produced thirteen more Champions. The Marbelton Boxers today have won well over 200 CCs.

STEYNMERE

Bruce and Margaret Cattanach's Steynmere Boxers have been prominent recently. Bruce comes from a Boxer family, as his mother was a Boxer breeder in the North East in the early days of the breed. Bruce once told me that the great Ringleader was used on one of the early Steynmere bitches, but there were no outstanding puppies in the litter. Bruce studied genetics at University, and his resulting career took him to the USA, where he earned the nickname of 'The Mouse Man'.

When he and Margaret returned to England they brought back a well-bred brindle and white Boxer, Black Rose of Cherokee Oaks, who became the foundation of the present-day Steynmere Boxers. In the early 1970s, Black Rose was mated to the great Picasso, who, more successful than Ringleader, sired the first, new, Steynmere Champion, Ritzi Miss. She was a great producer: her son, Summer Gold, was followed by Gold Mink and Moon Flame – all three were Champions. When Ritzi Miss was put to the Dutch import, Pirol von Belcane, she produced the super Ch. Steynmere Golden Link.

The top Steynmere Boxer, Night Rider, was very well-made, and a charming character – a Ritzi Miss grandson, who sired six Champions. Other Steynmere Champions were Garnet Gelert, Sharmdise Hustler and Forceful William. Altogether the Steynmere Boxers were responsible for 100 CCs. Dr Cattanach shows his dogs on a loose lead, and there is always an excellent rapport between him and his dogs.

SCOTTISH KENNELS

One of the early Scottish kennels was the BRAXBURN kennel, owned by Joan and Jimmy MacLaren. They had many Champions including Ch. Braxburn Flush Royal, Ch. Braxburn Waza Waza and Ch. Braxburn Its Dinah Might, Ch. Braxburn Cornelius, plus many other Braxburn Boxers who won at all levels in Scotland and England.

Lesley Boyle did a lot of winning with her CAMSAIL Boxers in Scotland, winning nearly twenty CCs. Ch. Camsail Lovebird was an extremely nice bitch.

Another well-known breeder and exhibitor in Scotland is Mrs Moray Bell, whose lovely Champion, MELVICHS Mellissa, won ten CCs. Another of her successful bitches was Miss Mudge.

Ch. Walkon Smash 'N Grab: Winner of four CCs, seven Reserve CCs, and Best in Show at the Working Breeds of Scotland Ch. Show.

Christine Duncan's ALLDANE Boxers have been very successful for Angela Kennett of the Trywell Boxers. Their Champions were Alldane Golden Wonder of Trywell and Alldane Golden Triumph of Trywell, who won more than twenty CCs between them.

A repeat mating of Ch. Tyegarth Famous Grouse produced another great Champion, Tyegarth Glenmorangie of Jenroy, bought in the nest by the lucky Jenny Townsend. He was the sire of six Champions including Carinya Rye 'n' Dry and two of the WALKON Champions, Walkon Smashed Again and Jenroy Pop My Cork to Walkon, who won the CC from the Veteran Class at Crufts in 1993. The extremely successful Walkon kennel is owned by Walker and Yvonne Miller, who, in the last few years, must have travelled thousands of miles to shows from their home in Scotland, to make up their many Champions, including Smashed Again, Going Dutch, and Slightly Sloshed, who, with her litter sister, Eddie and Helen Banks' Slightly Sozzled, were beautiful bitches by Grouse out of Mustang Wine.

It is impossible to mention all the top winners in the breed, but I think I must mention some of our great bitches. In his lifetime, a stud dog can sire very many puppies, but a bitch can only produce a limited number. Several of our Boxers have had two Champions. However, Christine Duncan's Alldane Golden Blossom, Odette of Arnogar, owned by Mrs Arnott and Mrs Garroway, Biloran Little Claret, owned by Bill and Ann Law, Panfield Party Piece of Greentub, and Mrs Norrington's Ch. Wardrobes Miss Sable produced three Champion Boxers each. But the accolade must go to Mrs Wiley's Ch. Wardrobes Silver Spurs and Helen Banks' Norwatch Mustang Wine, who both produced five Champions.

Chapter Seven

BUYING A PUPPY

There are many reasons why people are attracted to a certain breed of dog, and before you take on the responsibility of owning any dog, you must be sure that you can take care of that animal for the duration of its life. It is important to do as much research as possible into your chosen breed – reading books, talking to owners and breeders and attending shows – and then you can get down to the business of buying a puppy.

FINDING A BREEDER

The national Kennel Club keeps a list of all breeders, and will be able to provide you with a list of Boxer breeders – although they do not actually recommend individual breeders. Alternatively, you can get in touch with a Boxer breed club in your area.

Boxers puppies are irresistible, but you must be guided by your head as well as by your heart.

Once again, you can get the secretary's name and address, and probably the telephone number, from the Kennel Club. In my opinion, the names you get from a breed club secretary are more reliable, and you are more likely to be given a breeder who will suit your particular requirements.

The next step is to make an appointment to go and see one or more breeders. Hopefully they will have puppies for you to see, or perhaps a litter is due, and you can make an appointment for a later date. Most breeders have one or two (probably a few!) Boxers in the house. They may be current show dogs or pensioners, so you will have an opportunity to get to know these dogs, and to see if their characters appeal to you, and whether they are the kind of dogs you would like to own. Incidentally, do not expect an immaculate house! It is probably better not to take a huge crowd of family, friends and relations with you. This is the time to ask lots of the questions, and to get as much advice as possible from the breeder.

COLOUR

This is a matter of personal preference, and something you may well have decided on before you located a breeder. There are two colours, red and brindle. Red is not 'pillar box' red, but the shorthand for the sandy-brown colour. This can be any shade from light golden fawn to a dark deer red, rather like mahogany. Brindle means black stripes on a fawn background, and the fawn background can be any shade from golden to mahogany. The black stripes can be wide so that they cover much of the background or thin stripes so that plenty of the background colour can be seen. It is thought, in the show ring, that the black stripes should be well defined and evenly spread out, meeting in a chevron pattern on the back.

Both these colours, brindle or red, can have white markings. These white markings are normally on the feet, legs and the chest. They are sometimes on or round the neck, and are often on the head, between the eyes from the nose to the forehead (a blaze). These white markings should be even. A Boxer with white right over one eye or both eyes is mismarked, and the white must not cover more than one third of the whole dog.

Many Boxers are born white – remember the first Boxers were white – but these have been disallowed since 1924 in Breed Standards all over the world. This probably stems from the fact that the Boxers were used by the German Army in the trenches in the first World War as guards and for carrying telegraph cables from post to post in the trenches. And in the Second World War they were used as guard dogs. In both these activities, the white markings showed up and the dogs could be shot by a sniper. For this reason, the solid brindle colour was the best camouflage, so the white Boxer, and the white markings on a Boxer, were considered undesirable – and

The red and white coloured Tonantron Glory Lass, pictured at eight weeks. This pup went on to become Ch. Tonantron Glory Lass, the breed record holder.

Ch. Tonantron Glory Lass, pictured at fourteen months, just after winning her title.

this has influenced the Standard ever since. So, in most cases, your choice will be fawn or brindle, with white markings or without white markings.

Sometimes a breeder will try to find homes for white puppies, but this can prove problematical. A white pup should be sold for less money, and the prospective purchaser should be told that although white puppies are the same in all respects as their coloured littermates, they are not accepted in the Breed Standard, and such a dog cannot compete at a dog show. The British Breed Council do not advise keeping whites, and as all clubs abide by the Boxer Breed Council Code of Conduct, you may not be admitted as a member to a breed club if you own a white Boxer.

MALE OR FEMALE
The male Boxer is slightly taller than the bitch in height – two inches at the withers – and when adult and fully mature, the male is probably three or four inches wider. The main disadvantage in having a bitch as a family pet is coping with the seasons. At the time of her season, a bitch must not meet a male dog of any breed, because during her season she could become pregnant, so doors and gates must be kept closed at this time. A season lasts three weeks and happens twice a year. If you have the kind of family which can be trusted about doors, gates and windows, fair enough

Faerdorn Roosevelt of Wildax: The male Boxer is slightly taller and wider than the female.

Pearce.

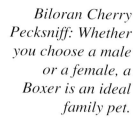

Biloran Cherry Pecksniff: Whether you choose a male or a female, a Boxer is an ideal family pet.

Pearce.

– but friends and visitors must also be considered. Males do not come into season, and although many people fear that a male will have a 'wander lust' and go straying after bitches in season, I have never encountered this problem. It is possible to have a bitch spayed and a dog castrated. I have never had any of my Boxers spayed or castrated, and I believe you should consult your vet about this. This must be your decision.

I have found that either sex of Boxer will make an ideal family pet. Personally, the Boxers I have loved most and who have given me the most devotion, have been males, although I have been fond of many of my bitches. But if I had to have just one Boxer, it would be a Boxer dog.

ASSESSING THE PUPPIES

When you have found a breeder who has a litter of puppies, be guided by the breeder as to what age to view the litter. Boxer pups are really nothing to look at at all until they are at least four weeks old, by which time they are standing up and beginning to play. Any time before that the pups are rather like slugs, crawling around, sleeping and feeding. At four weeks they begin to walk about, slowly and a bit uncertainly; they play with each other, and with the odd toy given to them, and by this time they

Skelder Much Ado (Skelder Saddler – Ch. Comedy of Errors of Skelder) and her puppy, Skelder Stage Struck, sired by Skelder Special Branch. When you are choosing a puppy, it is helpful if you can see one or both of the parents.

Biloran Miss Pipchin (Ch. Faerdorn Pheasant Plucker – Biloran Miss Whotzit), pictured as a youngster.

Pearce.

A puppy with cropped ears (which can be seen in America and on the Continent) looks very different, although the breed requirements for the shape of the head are identical.

are barking as well as crying. They are quite interesting to watch – in fact they are great time wasters! It will be just possible to speculate how they will turn out as adults, but it will still be another four or five weeks before show quality and construction can be ascertained.

Try to see the mother of the pups, and the father if you can. It is sometimes more difficult to see the father, as he may be a well-known stud dog living some way away, but it might be possible to see a photograph and you may be told about his character. With a family, dog character is more important than looks and show prospects. Of course, you will be able to develop your Boxer's character to fit your own family and the life you lead, but I feel you must have the basic, charming character to start off with, on which to base your training.

By the time the puppies are eight weeks old, their individual characters are emerging. There is the 'thinking' puppy, the adventurous pup, the 'digger', the noisy, demanding pup, and the quiet, loving pup who snuggles up to you for attention. This is the ideal age to buy a puppy, as not only can you get some idea of personality, you will also have a puppy that is willing to change environments. I have found that after fourteen weeks, Boxer puppies do not change homes quite so easily. They feel rejected by their first family, who have bred them, and so take longer to settle with their new family.

I also feel that any of the teenage years (up to two to two-and-a-half years) are very bad times for a Boxer to change homes. A dog of this age can feel utterly

Ch. Fletcher of Sunhawk Norwatch (Ch. Mitchum of Sunhawk Norwatch – Glenfall Hit the Heights at Tynteville) pictured at four months.

Banks.

rejected, and may turn into a juvenile delinquent. If you want an adult Boxer, wait until the dog is fully mature and then it is more likely to cope with the change of home.

There is some controversy as to whether potential purchasers should see the whole litter, or just the puppy which is for sale. I can see both sides of the argument. When a prospective Boxer owner is faced with a litter of puppies, they are sometimes completely overwhelmed! They pick up all the puppies, forgetting which one they liked a few minutes ago, and get thoroughly confused. So, if you have said that you are looking for a red and white dog, and the breeder comes into the room with an appealing red and white dog, and it sits on your lap and snuggles up to you and nibbles your ear, then you will probably decide that this is the puppy for you, and forget that there may have been others in the litter, others that you might have liked a bit more!

The breeder may want to retain a particular puppy as a show prospect, but very often, when a breeder tells a client that a puppy is being retained, that is the puppy the client wants, and if he or she cannot have it, a sale is lost. I remember many years ago, my friend 'Cookie' and I saw a litter of very nice pups at the Gremlin kennel, and six months later, we saw a new Gremlin puppy enter the show ring, whose date of birth tied in exactly with the litter we had seen. Cookie muttered "I'm sure we did not see that one, it was probably shut in the bedroom!"

So, I am afraid, you will have to go along with the breeder's routine when seeing puppies. Try to think how the owner of the litter feels about that litter. She has seen each puppy born, helped many of them into the world, dried them and heard their first cry as the puppy took its first breath, watched it taking its first steps, and been with it and its brothers and sisters through good and naughty times, seen it through the weaning process, and now you are going to take over and be responsible for the rest of that Boxer's life. Not only are you taking on a new life to mix with your family, but you are taking away a very precious life from someone who has been responsible for it until now. Try to bear this in mind.

You will probably be asked a lot of questions, so that the breeder can be as certain as possible that the home you are going to give will be a loving, permanent home. Be prepared to pay a reasonable asking price; it is not common practice to bargain about the price of a pup.

KEEPING MORE THAN ONE BOXER
Another of your decisions may be whether you want to keep more than one dog at a time. A pair of Boxer puppies is not advisable. They are twice as much trouble as a single puppy, they are twice as difficult to manage, and they are twice as naughty! Mind you, I have known of a few perfect pairs, but on the whole this is rare.

Ch. Biloran Miss Nancy and Biloran Miss Pipchin, pictured as a puppy. If you want a second Boxer, wait until your first Boxer is mature before acquiring a puppy.

Pearce.

After starting with just one Boxer bitch, a sole and constant companion, we have had much fun and amusement with a pair – mother and daughter – and they were perfect companions to each other. However, I never felt that I was quite as important, as the two dogs just loved each other. I think the most perfect combination if you want two Boxers, and you have the time and space, is to get your second one, a puppy, when the first one is between four and six years old. At this time, the older dog is not too old to put up with a wild, new puppy. In fact, the first dog will probably get a new lease of life, and the baby will pick up most of the older dog's good habits – so you may have the perfect pair.

It is inadvisable to keep more than two Boxers at a time, unless you are running a kennel. The pack instinct comes out when many dogs are kept together. For someone who has had thirty adults and several litters at the same time, this may seem a mad thing to say; but unless you want to go in for dog breeding as a full time profession, do not have more than two Boxers at a time. In my opinion, dogs in a pack are not all that happy, and, certainly, you will miss the devotion of your pet dog and companion.

COLLECTING YOUR PUPPY
When you have arranged to collect your Boxer puppy, it will probably be about eight weeks old. Make sure you arrive on time, as the breeder will not want to send the puppy away just after a meal, and will have adjusted the routine accordingly. Ideally, a gap of four hours should be left between feeding and travelling.

It is a good idea to bring a rug, an old towel and some kitchen paper towels with you. Some pups are sick when travelling, and they may suffer from this for the rest of their lives. Others take to the car from Day One – it all depends on the individual dog. However, the first car journey is more likely to cause some upset, and there is little you can do except clear up the mess, and remain calm and composed. If car sickness continues to be a problem, consult your vet and, under his direction, try some anti-sickness tablets until you find the right one.

When you collect your puppy, you should be given a pedigree, which will give your dog's family tree, usually going back three generations. The Champions will be written in red or underlined. You should also get the Kennel Club registration form, and in the UK many breeders provide insurance for the first week or two. A diet sheet will also be provided, which you should follow carefully. You should also be given a list of dates when the puppy was wormed, and the medication used for the worming. If you have small children, it is very important that your puppy is wormed regularly. Consult your vet as to what worming schedule you should follow.

If you are collecting your puppy at eight weeks of age, it is unlikely to have had any inoculations. You will, therefore, need to discuss with your vet when inoculations for the pup should be given. Vets have different ideas about this, and this may depend on the locality, so be guided by your vet.

ARRIVING HOME

When you arrive home, your puppy will find everything very strange and bewildering, so give it time to settle down and get used to the new smells and the feel of its new home. Do not fuss your puppy too much, but allow it to explore, and introduce the pup to the garden and to its sleeping quarters. The breeder will probably have given you some food, so that the the puppy's first meal will be something it is used to eating. Make sure your puppy is not disturbed while it is eating. It is a good thing if the breeder gives you a toy or a small piece of bedding, as this will help your puppy to feel at home straightaway. Try to remember that there is nothing quite so traumatic as a puppy going to a new home. The pup has never been alone before – it has always had its brothers and sisters to snuggle up with – and so it will feel very lonely to begin with. So, as well as caring for your new puppy, you and your family will have to provide love and companionship, taking the place of its canine family.

Companionship at night will be the most difficult thing to tackle. The first night you have your puppy, it may be so fatigued with coping with all the new experiences that it goes off into a deep sleep, and you think all is well. The next night, after a day

Your Boxer puppy will feel very strange when it first arrives home, and you should give it time to explore its new surroundings.

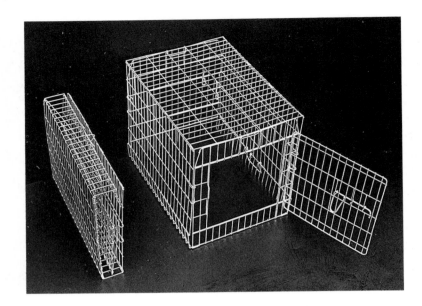

An indoor kennel is an invaluable item of equipment for a new puppy. It provides a quiet, safe place for periods of rest, and it also helps with the house training. It should never be used as a punishment.

of playing and getting used to its new home, the crying will probably start. There are two methods to adopt. The first is to take the puppy's bed into your bedroom and put it beside your bed. The bed should be warm, lined with a blanket, plus a covered hot-water bottle. The puppy will be reassured because it is not on its own, and will probably settle down to sleep. After a couple of weeks when the puppy is really at home, the bed can be moved outside the bedroom, on the landing, and eventually into the kitchen or wherever you want your puppy to sleep.

The other method is to put the pup in the kitchen, or wherever you want your puppy to sleep, put in ear-plugs and harden your heart. I always adopt the first method, as I hate to think of an unhappy Boxer, crying out of loneliness. I have found that if the puppy has another dog – or even a cat – to sleep with, it will settle much more quickly. If the puppy is not disturbed in the night, it can go through the night without needing to relieve itself – even when it is only eight or nine weeks old. However, I always put a few newspapers round the bed, just in case. Of course I always put the puppy out just before bedtime, and it is sometimes better to feed a solid meal last thing, rather than a milky one. In America, it is common practice to purchase an indoor kennel or crate when you buy your puppy. This is very useful for the puppy while it is small; it provides a place where the puppy can rest undisturbed, the puppy can be left safely when you have to go out – without the risk of chewing – and it helps when you are house training your puppy.

You should always have fresh water available for your dog. You will probably be giving your puppy four meals a day to begin with, two meaty meals and two milky meals. One of the milky meals can be stopped when the puppy is roughly three months old. It is not thought all that important for a Boxer to have a great deal of milk once it is weaned from its mother. After six months of age, the other milk meal can be cut out, so your dog is on two solid meals a day, but the total amount of food must be gradually increased. All my adult Boxers have two meals a day, because I think it is such a long time for a dog to go with just one meal a day, but that is a matter of personal preference.

Change the number of meals gradually, and I do not advise you to stick to exact times for meals; your puppy must fit in with your family and your life style. However, you should make sure that the family pays attention to the rights of the dog. In other words, try to stop the children waking the puppy up when it has just dropped off to sleep. In fact, when the puppy is small, you must make sure that it has plenty of sleep and rest during the day. A healthy puppy will never give up, it will play until it drops. I always put the pup in its bed for quiet rest at least twice a day. A very rough guide to a puppy's age is that a week is the equivalent to a month of a baby, so do not expect too much from a baby puppy.

It is better not to take your puppy for walks until it is at least six months old, and it is essential that you do not allow your dog to foul the pavements or places where people walk or children play. At this age, it is a good idea to enrol in a dog training class. Try to find a class where instruction in basic obedience is given. Unless you have bought a show quality puppy, and you intend to take in the show circuit, it is not worth getting involved with show training

HOUSE TRAINING

House training a Boxer is very easy, and it can probably be accomplished in a few days. It is far easier in the summer when all the doors into the garden can be left open permanently, but Boxer puppies are quick to catch on, and will soon understand what is expected, and will soon learn to use the same place for toilet purposes. Novice owners sometimes complain, saying "he did not go to the door and bark to be let out." Perhaps the owner did not notice the puppy walking past the door, or hovering about near the door. The essential ingredient in house training is prompt help from the owner, who must be on the alert at all times. If a puppy makes a 'mistake', it is often the fault of the owner for not being sufficiently vigilant.

The Boxer *wants* to be clean. For generations, the Boxer has been a house dog, a companion dog, brought up in the house close to people, rather than being kept in the corner of a stable yard. So a Boxer does not like to live in a messy house, and as soon as a puppy learns the right place, it will go out and use the same place every time. It is up to you to show your puppy what is required.

Ch. Jacquet's Cambridge Fortune: This young bitch took the American show scene by storm.

Chapter Eight

THE ADULT BOXER

Officially and technically, a Boxer or any breed of dog, ceases to be a puppy at a year old. However, a Boxer takes a great deal longer to grow up. I have heard it said that a Boxer remains a puppy until the day he dies of old age, and most Boxers are certainly middle-aged before they stop behaving like puppies.

For at least two years, Boxers have to be fed as though they are still growing. In fact, they do actually grow bigger for at least two to three years. The height is decided by eighteen months, but an adult will continue to develop, particularly in width, for the next couple of years. A well cared for, correctly fed, energetic Boxer should never be fat, but during this time the muscles develop, and the dog becomes thicker, heavier and wider. When a three or four-year-old Boxer hurls himself at you in a playful dash, you know you have been hit!

A gregarious Boxer, who loves people, and expects all the world to reciprocate, has to be trained to control his exuberance! This is not easy – and almost impossible if you have more than one Boxer. So, it is advisable to have one Boxer at a time, or at least make sure that you find time to train your puppy on its own, away from dogs, children, and any other distractions.

COMPANIONSHIP

As your puppy gets older, your Boxer will be trustworthy enough to be allowed the run of the house; but being a companion dog, it will always want and need companionship. A Boxer does not like to be left alone for too long, and would far rather accompany you wherever you are going. A well trained Boxer is a delightful companion, and it will probably feel that it has come with you even if left in the car. However, I should warn you that a great deal of damage can be done to the interior of a car by a full-grown, bored Boxer. I would recommend that you fit your car with a well-made, strong dog guard. A bored dog is likely to find its own amusement, and that could well result in destructive behaviour. A Boxer puppy, and, I suspect, a puppy of any breed, likes to be entertained. A Boxer puppy sits on the floor at your feet, looking up at you with an expectant expression, waiting for you to do something – play, talk, go out for a walk – anything that will be interesting and stimulating. As you are his human companion, you have a duty towards him.

ADULT FEEDING

Once your Boxer is an adult, make sure that it has fresh water to drink, which is readily available. I usually feed my Boxers twice a day – one meal is a snack, the other a main meal. I do this because it must be awfully boring for a dog to have nothing to think about all day or to look forward to for twenty-four hours.

A puppy or youngster has to have plenty of food of the best quality while growing, but once up to size, this amount can be cut back to about 1lb meat per day and 1/2lb

Jacquet's Jersey Trooper, pictured at nine months. The Boxer is a sociable dog and thrives on human companionship

of biscuit, rice or pasta, divided into two meals. If your Boxer is living outside, doing some work, going to shows or taking part in Obedience competitions, a little more food, in the form of protein, will be needed to keep the dog in peak condition.

If your Boxer bitch has been spayed, she may have a tendency to put on extra weight. Your vet will be able to advise you on how much food she should have. Keep a sharp eye on your bitch's shape, and if you see her getting fat, go back to your vet. A Boxer who has passed middle age and is fat, is not a well or happy Boxer, so it is important to do something. Like some people, some Boxers are inclined to put on weight more easily than others – it is in their make-up. I have a little bitch, called Feather, who gets fat at the sight, smell, or thought of food! I can only keep her the right shape by almost starving her. She gets a small handful of biscuit and a very small piece of cooked meat twice a day – a minute amount for a big breed, and about half the amount my other Boxers have each day. She is perfectly happy and I am determined to keep her in shape. She is now eleven years old.

The Boxer tummy is not easy to deal with. I do not know why – although I have heard many theories, such as too much acid, stress, nervous energy, wind or worry. I have found that each Boxer is different, and different things either suit or disagree with them. Experiment – and when you find something that a particular Boxer likes and it keeps him in good nick, stick to that and feed the same food every day. Dogs are not like humans, needing a change of diet. They are far better if fed with the same food every day if it suits them.

GROOMING

Most healthy, correctly fed Boxers need the minimum of grooming, and a brush every day is probably enough. A rubber glove (the type used for washing-up or housework) is useful for removing loose hairs, and this is invaluable when your Boxer is moulting. It is always nice to see a shiny coat, but, in fact, a slightly duller waterproof coat is more correct. A short-coated Boxer only needs one or two baths a year – at the beginning of the summer, and if your dog rolls in something disgusting! There are many good dog shampoos on the market. Some insecticidal shampoos need to be left to dry on the dog, so make sure you choose a warm, sunny day. Other shampoos have to be rinsed out, and then you must be careful to dry the dog thoroughly. If you have any problems with your Boxer's coat, consult your vet.

If you are competing with your Boxer in the show ring, your dog will need to be bathed a couple of days before the show. It is also common practice to trim your Boxer. This involves trimming the long hairs around the muzzle, on the eyebrows, and on 'beauty spots' on the cheeks and under the chin. The edges down the back of

Ch. Tonantron All Glory of Wildax: An impressive example of a sound, well-cared for Boxer.

Pearce.

the hindlegs, and down the side of the neck are other areas which can be trimmed. This should be done with sharp scissors, working downwards, the way the hair grows, so that the outline is left smooth with no jagged edges.

TEETH

Teeth should be kept clean. Actually, I have never had a dog who has needed to have its teeth cleaned, but if this is neccessary there are specially manufactured canine toothbrushes and toothpastes on the market. I prefer to provide marrow bones or nylabones for my dogs to chew on.

EARS

The inside of your Boxer's ears must be kept clean, and this can be done by wiping out each ear with a thin clean cloth or cotton wool. If your dog has dirty ears, your vet will recommend a suitable ear lotion. However, be careful not to probe too deeply into the ear. Leave that to your vet, who knows exactly what to do, and will not cause any damage. A vet can also deal with mites which can get into the ear and cause infection.

EYES

Boxer puppies often develop droopy eyes when they are teething. This is because the back teeth are located very close to the eyes, so drooping eyelids may persist throughout the teething period, until the dog is eighteen months of age. There is nothing you can do with loose lower eyelids at this time, although a good-quality eye-dropper can be used. In the winter make sure that your Boxer does not lie staring into an open fire for too long, as this can irritate the eyes. In the summer you should prevent your dog from leaning out of the car window when you are travelling, as pollen or grass seeds can cause irritation to the eyes.

NAILS

A Boxer's nails should be kept short. A puppy's nails can be cut by using blunt-ended scissors. All you need to do is to remove the very sharp white tip. Be careful that you do not cut the quick or the nail will bleed. Later, as the dog grows, the nails thicken and so strong clippers will be needed. A dog that is walked regularly on roads and pavements usually has well manicured nails. Incidentally, a Boxer who has the correct tight, catlike feet often has short nails.

EXERCISE

An adult Boxer does not *need* a great deal of exercise to stay fit and healthy. However, most Boxers enjoy the stimulation of going out, and will keep going until the owner has had enough! The ideal routine is a couple of walks a day, and I find it immensely rewarding to see a dog enjoying the exercise, seeing new things, going to new places, meeting new people and dogs. In these situations a dog's mind is alert, and it is interested in everything that is going on. It is a good idea to do something with your dog each time you go for a walk. Let your Boxer carry something for you, or let it retrieve a ball – in fact, anything to occupy its mind. Go for different walks and vary the routine, and this will all help to keep your Boxer entertained.

BASIC OBEDIENCE

For one hundred years, the Boxer has been one of the most trainable breed of dog; the word tractable was translated from the first Munich Standard, and that word means trainable, easy to train and eager to understand what is required. So you are a step ahead anyway. This training has to start as early as possible and of course be done with extreme kindness. Keep at it and you will be amazed at what your Boxer can learn.

A few basic principles have to be learnt by you, the owner, such as always using the same words for what you want your Boxer to do: the same encouraging, kind tone of voice and plenty of praise, patting and hugging when something is accomplished. Another thing to remember is that a young puppy can only pay attention for a very short time, so for the first few training sessions, as soon as your puppy is tired, and begins to flag, pack up at once. You will also find that new events, new places and the excitement of seeing other new dogs, takes a lot out of a puppy, so it will feel tired very quickly. A young Boxer should not be taken out for a proper walk until it is at least six months old. A youngster will get enough exercise playing about in the house and garden. In the garden, you can teach your Boxer to walk on a lead properly, at the right speed for you, to walk to heel, not to pull, to stop when told to, and to sit close beside you at your feet. Puppy socialisation classes are becoming increasingly popular, and these are an important learning experience for the young Boxer. You can take your puppy along to these as soon as the inoculation programme has been completed.

You can then graduate to a dog training class. Most Boxers find these great fun, and your chief task will be to stop your dog from getting over-excited and behaving like an idiot! However, once your Boxer settles down after a couple of sessions, it can be taught a great deal. Mind you, you should have a trainer who understands the Boxer character. Some trainers think the Boxer's exuberance and sense of fun can disrupt a whole class, and they prefer the more subservient and passive breeds.

Try to find a training class which teaches basic obedience, plus the Kennel Club's Good Citizen Scheme. This scheme was first started in America a couple of years ago, teaching both dog and owner to be Good Citizens, so that dogs will be more acceptable to the general public. The Good Citizen Scheme trains you and your dog in very basic obedience, nothing very complicated, and at the end of a simple, non-competitive course, you and your dog are awarded a certificate and so become Good Citizens. Many training classes also teach show training, how to stand your dog to show to the best advantage, and how to move at the correct speed – in this instance you must fit in with the dog's natural pace. The dog will also get used to being examined by strangers. If you have bought your Boxer as a show prospect, these classes are invaluable. However, if your interest is confined to basic training, it is not worth getting involved in this area. You are better off working towards becoming a Good Citizen with your dog. This is great fun and can be very rewarding.

CHOKE CHAINS
Choke chains are invaluable for training and Obedience work, but never leave one on your Boxer because the dog can choke if the chain gets caught on anything. There have been cases when the chain has caught at the top of wire when the dog was jumping up trying to get out of the run. There have also been cases when two

Boxers are an intelligent and athletic breed and can be trained to compete in Obedience and agility competitions. Yoneek Romance (Tyegarth Hiram Walker is Yooneek – Ryan's Daughter is Yooneek), known as Bella, has competed with Border Collies and the other more popular agility breeds, and has come out on top!
Bred by Valerie Tripe, owned by Peter and Lyn Durkin.

dogs have been playing, and the teeth of one dog have caught in the chain of the other, and the consequences have been horrific. So, if you plan to use a choke chain, make sure it is only worn when you are training your dog.

BARKING

The Boxer is not a barking dog, although most Boxers will bark for a good reason, if something is wanted urgently or if it senses something strange or suspicious. In fact, a common complaint is that the Boxer, bought as a guard, does not bark enough! One new lady owner once rang up to ask if there was anything wrong with her Boxer, bought as a replacement for a Cairn Terrier, because the Boxer did not bark at all. "My other little dog barked all the time, at everything, birds flying over and aeroplanes, it was so companoniable," she said. That is not at all Boxer!

The Boxer's guarding instinct does not develop until the dog is at least eighteen months old. There are many stories about adult Boxers silently letting burglars into a house, only for the burglar, thinking that he has found a fool of a friendly dog, to find himself pinned into the corner of a room, and not allowed to move until the owner comes to see what the clever Boxer has caught! The Boxer is a thinking dog, who uses a certain amount of reasoning power. The reasoning may not be the same as yours, but there is nearly always thought behind the action, rather than just an impulse. It is you, the owner, who should teach the best way of reasoning.

JUMPING UP

Many Boxers have a habit of jumping up, and this is undesirable in a big, athletic breed. However, it is a natural trait for a Boxer. Small cattle herding dogs, such as Corgis, control the cattle by nipping at or around their feet. The Boxer is from Bull-baiting breeds, so it naturally jumps upwards to attack the beast's head, trying to latch on to the nose between the nostrils. So, at the drop of a hat, the Boxer jumps up to greet people. Breaking a Boxer of jumping upwards – its natural habit – is extremely difficult. I think the best thing to do is to start early, at only a few weeks of age. Do not encourage the puppy to come up towards you, but gently and firmly push the pup back on to the floor. Hopefully, the Boxer will understand that you do not approve of jumping up. If your puppy persists in this habit as it gets older, you must respond by pushing the dog down, very firmly. Hold the dog down on the floor for a few seconds saying "Down" in a firm, deep voice. I have been told that when a dog jumps up, if you step hard on its back feet, that will make it go down. This can be difficult to do and is unkind to the dog. You will have to persist with all these 'cures' until you find the one which works for you and your Boxer.

FIGHTS

There is no denying that when two or three Boxers are gathered together, there is a tendency to come to blows. Males usually fight for a reason: competing for a bitch, a treasured possession, or for their owner's affections. Bitches, on the other hand, seem to fight just because they want to, and they will keep going until the bitter end, unless prevented. They attack the front legs, head and chest. Males usually fight standing up, going for the head and throat, and they make a lot more noise.

Generally, at some stage in the fight there will be a slight pause, and at that point it may be possible to stop the fight and part the dogs. Once the dogs are separated, go over the two dogs carefully, checking that they have not got any tooth puncture marks. If these heal too quickly, they can fester, so they must be kept open and clean. If the wounds are serious, veterinary attention may be needed. Preventing a fight before it starts is obviously preferable. Observation is imperative when keeping dogs, and I do not recommend that Boxers are kept in large numbers.

RESPONSIBLE OWNERSHIP

When you own a Boxer, not only do you have a duty to the Boxer, but you and the Boxer also have a duty to other people. So we, the dog lovers, must try to counteract the anti-dog feeling which persists at this time. It is up to us to have dogs which have been taught not to foul pavements, grass verges or places where people walk, or where children play. We must try to teach our dogs not to bark excessively and continuously, and not to attack people in play, as some non-dog people cannot tell a mock attack from a real one. It is important to remember that to some people, and certainly to small children, a Boxer may seem big and menacing, so let us make sure that we, our family and Boxers, become Good Citizens.

Anatomy of the Boxer

illustrated by
Ch. Biloran Miss Nancy,
a beautifully
constructed Boxer.

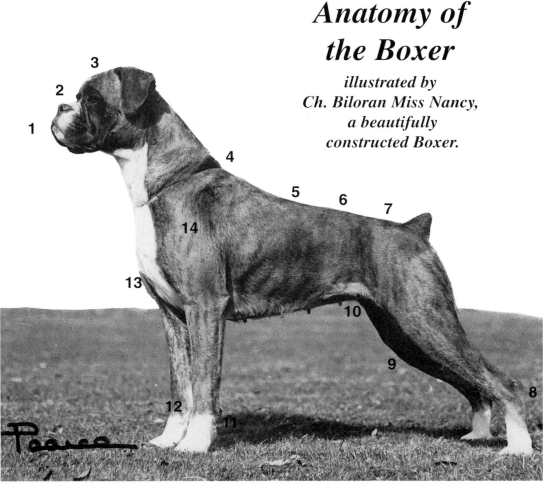

Key

1. Muzzle	6. Loin	11. Front pastern
2. Stop	7. Croup	12. Pastern joint
3. Occiput	8. Hock joint	13. Fore Chest
4. Withers	9. Stifle	14. Shoulder
5. Back	10. Tuck up	

Chapter Nine

THE BREED STANDARD

DRAWING UP A STANDARD

I wonder if any other Breed Standard has gone through the many traumatic stages the Boxer Standard has had to endure? Right from the start of the breed in the 1890s, there have been differences of opinion between the people who were pioneering the Boxer and trying to decide on a Standard for the breed. The original Munich Boxer Club broke up or was dissolved at least twice, or maybe three times, because of disagreements most probably over the Standard! These early pioneers found it hard to agree on the dog they were trying to breed – what it should look like, the type of character to aim for, and more importantly, how to achieve the desired results.

It is extremely difficult to describe an animal in words, especially a dog that is so lively and unique. Everyone probably had slightly differing views on different aspects of the dog – as they do today – and these views are held very strongly by each individual. No wonder tempers were frayed and clubs dissolved! However, those early pioneers were tenacious. They felt strongly about the importance of the breed which they were inventing, and so they reassembled, and the Munich Boxer Club was reformed.

As there were other groups of enthusiasts in Southern Germany, the breed was never abandoned, and by 1896 a St Bernard Dog Club was asked to schedule a class for Boxers at a show, and a dog called Flocki was persuaded to enter. Being the only dog in the class, Flocki won the first class for Boxers at a show, so became Boxer No. 1 in the Stud Book being compiled by the Munich Boxer Club. This Stud Book was also to include a Standard for the Breed.

So that was the start. The Munich Boxer Club had a Boxer entered in the Stud Book and the beginnings of a Standard. That first Standard, which was approved in 1900, did not change a great deal over the next few years. Gradually, all the other

Quibas van Rusticana of Wildax: A Dutch import to Frank and Margaret Wildman's Wildax kennel. This powerfully built Boxer has the cropped ears, which are desirable in America and on the Continent.

clubs and groups of Boxer enthusiasts approved this Standard, and it became unified throughout Germany and surrounding countries. So by about the 1920s it is possible to say that all Boxer breeders were adhering to the same Standard, which had just been thoroughly revised. In 1924 all completely black or pure white Boxers were excluded, and later in 1925, checks were banned. It was also at this time, too, after a great deal of negotiating, that the Munich Boxer Club was able to get the Boxer recognised as an official working Police Dog, which the breed still is to this day.

THE BOXER STANDARD

Drawn up in still valid form in 1905, this Standard was thoroughly revised in 1920.

1. GENERAL APPEARANCE: The Boxer is a medium-sized, smooth-haired, sturdy dog of short, square build and strong bone. The musculation is clean (dry) and powerfully developed and stands out plastically (pliantly) through the skin. The movements are lively and full of strength and nobility. The Boxer should not appear plump or heavy, lean or racy.

A typical British Boxer head, illustrated by Ch. Jenroy Pop My Cork to Walkon: Winner of 20 CCs, 23 Reserve CCs, one Group (all breeds Ch. Show), three Reserve Groups (Ch. Shows), Dog CC at Crufts 1990 and 1993 from the veteran class.

2. HEAD: The head imparts to the Boxer a unique, individual stamp. It must be in good proportion to the body and should appear neither too light nor too heavy. The skull should be as lean and angular as possible, without salient cheeks, the muzzle as broad and massive as possible. The beauty of the head depends on the harmonious proportion between the muzzle and the skull. From whatever direction the head is viewed, whether from the front, from the top or from the side, the muzzle must always appear in correct relationship to the skull, that is, it must never seem too small. It should be clean (dry), showing neither wrinkles nor dewlap. Folds normally appear on the forehead when the ears are erect and they are always indicated from the foot of the nose running downward on both sides of the muzzle. The dark mask is confined to the muzzle and must be in distinct contrast to the colour of the head, so that the face will not have a sombre expression.

The muzzle is powerfully developed in all three dimensions, thus it must not be

Tito del Colle dell Infinito: An excellent Boxer head of the Continental type.

This dell Infinito Boxer shows the correct head with a well balanced muzzle to skull. Lip placement extremely good, eye excellent shape and expression superb in a plain black face, which is very rare, especially in Britain.

pointed or narrow, short or shallow. Its shape is influenced first through the formation of both jawbones, second through the placement of the teeth in the jawbones and third through the quality of the lips.

The two jawbones do not end in a perpendicular plane in front, but the lower jaw protrudes beyond the upper and curves slightly upward. The Boxer is normally undershot. The upper jaw is broad where attached to the skull and maintains this breadth, except for a very slight tapering to the front. Thus both jaws are very wide in front. The canine teeth should be as widely separated as possible, the incisors (6) should all be in one row, with no projection of the middle teeth. In the upper jaw they are set in a line curving slightly forward, in the lower jaw they should be in a straight line. The bite is powerful and sound, the teeth set in the most normal arrangement possible.

*The correct undershot jaw
required by the Boxer
Breed Standard.*

The shape of the muzzle is completed by the lips. The upper lip is thick and padded, filling out the frontal space created by the projection of the lower jaw and is supported by the fangs (canines) of the lower jaw. These fangs must therefore stand as far apart as possible and be of good length so that the front surface of the muzzle becomes almost square, forming an obtuse angle with the topline of the muzzle. The lower edge of the upper lip rests on the edge of the lower lip. The repandous part of the lower jaw, with the lower lip, called the chin, must not rise in front of the upper lip, but even less may it disappear under it. It must however be plainly perceptible when viewed from the front as well as from the side, without protruding and bending upward as in the Bulldog. The teeth of the lower jaw must not be visible when the mouth is closed, neither should the Boxer show its tongue when the mouth is closed.

The top of the skull is slightly arched, not so short as to be rotund, nor too flat, nor too broad and the occiput not too pronounced. The forehead forms a distinct stop with the topline of the muzzle. The bridge of the nose should not be forced back into the forehead like that of the Bulldog, nor should it slope down, however. The proportion between the length of the nose and that of the skull is as one (1) is to two (2). The tip of the nose lies somewhat higher than the root of the muzzle. The forehead shows a suggestion of furrow which however should not be too deep, especially between the eyes. The cheeks are powerfully developed to correspond with the strong bite, without protruding from the head with too bulgy an appearance.

Sp. Ch. Janos de Loermo of Lynpine. The Boxer standard is full of contradictions: Furrowing of forehead should only appear when alert; cheeks should be well developed but not protruding. Folds always on both sides of muzzle and nose broad, black and turned up. The contradictions make it so difficult to breed a Boxer head.

They should preferably taper into the muzzle in a slight curve. The ears are set on high, are cropped to a sharp point, fairly long, without too broad a shell and are carried perpendicular. The eyes are dark, not too small or protruding and not deep set. They disclose an expression of energy and intelligence but should not appear gloomy, threatening or piercing. The eyes must have a dark rim. The nose is broad and black, very slightly turned up, the nostrils wide, with the naso-labial line between them.

FAULTS: Lack of nobility and expression, sombre face, unserviceable bite due to disease or faulty tooth placement, Pinscher or Bulldog head, drivelling, badly cropped ears, unpigmented third eyelid, showing teeth or tongue, light (bird of prey) eyes, sloping topline of the muzzle (downface), snipy bite or muzzle too light, brown, flesh-coloured or pink nose.

3. NECK: Round, not too short and thick but of ample length, yet strong, muscular and clean cut throughout, without dewlap. It runs down to the back in an elegant arch with distinctly marked nape. FAULTS: Dewlap.

4. BODY: The body is square. The profile or outline, that is a horizontal line over the back and two vertical lines, the one touching the forechest in front, the other the ischiatic bones in the rear, form with the ground level a square. The torso rests on sturdy straight legs with strong bones.

5. CHEST AND FOREQUARTERS: The chest is deep, reaching down to the elbows. The depth of the chest amounts to half the height of the dog at the withers. The ribs are well arched but not barrel shaped, extending far to the rear. The loins are short, closed and taut and slightly tucked up. The lower stomach line blends into an elegant curve to the rear. The shoulders are long and sloping, close lying but not excessively covered with muscle. The upper arm is long, forming a right angle to the shoulder blade. The forelegs when seen from the front must be straight, stand parallel to each other and have strong, firmly articulated bones. The elbows must not press too closely to the chest wall nor stand off too far. The forearm is perpendicular, long and firmly muscled. The pastern joint of the foreleg is short, clearly defined but not distended. The pastern is short, slightly slanting but stands almost perpendicular to the ground. Feet are small with tightly arched toes (cat feet) and hard soles.
FAULTS: Too broad and low in front, loose shoulders, chest hanging between the shoulders, hare feet, hollow flanks, hanging stomach, turned legs and toes.

6. BACK: The withers should be clearly defined; the whole back short, straight, broad and strongly muscled.
FAULTS: Carp (roach) back, sway back, thin, lean back, long, narrow sharp sunken in loins, weak union with croup.

7. HINDQUARTERS: Very strongly muscled, the musculation hard as a board and standing out very plastically (pliantly) through the skin. The thighs are not narrow and flat but are broad and curved. The breech musculation is as strongly developed.
   The croup slightly sloped, with a flat arch and broad. Tail set on high rather than too low, tail docked and carried upward. The pelvis should be long and, in bitches especially, broad. Upper and lower thigh long, hip and knee joint with as much angle as possible. In a standing position the knee should reach so far forward that it would meet a vertical line drawn from the hip protuberance to the floor. The hock angle about 140 degrees, the lower part of the foot at a slight slope of 95-100 degrees to the floor, thus not completely vertical. Seen from behind the hind legs should be straight. The hock joints clean, not distended, with powerful heels, the toes normally slightly longer than in front but similar in all other respects.
FAULTS: Falling off or too arched or narrow croup, low set tail, overbuilt (higher in

back than in front), steep, stiff, insufficiently angulated hindquarters, light thighs, cow hocks, bow or sickle legs, narrow heels, hind dewclaws, soft hocks, tottering, waddling gait, hare feet, hindquarters too far under or too far behind.

8. HEIGHT: Males 57-63 cm at the withers, Females 53-59 cm. The height is measured with the dog standing erect and the measurement is taken with a straight edge from the withers, along the elbow down to the ground.

9. MASS: A male of about 60 cm should be over 30 kg, females of about 56 cm should weigh about 25 kg.

10. COAT: Short and glossy, lying smooth and tight to the body.

11. COLOUR: The colours are fawn and brindle. Fawn occurs in various shades, from dark deer red to light yellow, the shades in between (red fawn) are however the most beautiful. The mask is black, but must be confined to the muzzle so that the face does not appear sombre or unfriendly.

The brindle variety has dark or black stripes running parallel to the ribs, on a fawn

BRINDLE MARKINGS

Golden Brindle: Ch. Wildax Silver showing brindle markings on a fawn background.

Mahogany Brindle: Biloran Louisa Chick showing brindle markings on a darker background.

Pearce.

Dark Brindle: Ch. Fletcher of Sunhawk Norwatch showing more pronounced brindle markings, but the two colours are still distinct.

Banks.

ground colour in the above shades. The stripes should be in distinct contrast to the ground colour, neither too close together nor too thinly dispersed. The ground colour must not be dirty and the two colours should not be intermingled (grizzled) so that the brindle markings disappear. White markings are not to be rejected; they are often very attractive in appearance. Unattractive white markings, such as a completely or laterally white head, etc., are faults.

All Boxers with any other colour, as well as those with the ground colour more than one third replaced by white, are not according to the Standard.

12. CHARACTER: The character of the Boxer is of the greatest importance and demands the most solicitous attention. He is renowned from olden times for his great love and loyalty for his master and the whole household, his alertness and fearless courage as a defender and protector. He is harmless in the family but distrustful of strangers, bright and friendly of temperament at play, but fearsome when roused. He is easily trained due to his obedience, his self-assurance and courage, his natural sharpness and scenting ability. Because of his modesty and cleanliness he is equally desirable as a family dog and a guard, escort or service dog. He is honest and loyal, never false or treacherous even in his old age.

FAULTS: Viciousness, treachery, unreliability, lack of temperament and cowardice.
The Boxer Club E.V. Sitz Munchen 1895 The Boxer Standard (No. 144b FC1).

In the 1920s the Boxer became popular in the United States, and dogs were being imported from Europe. It became clear that some of the imports from Austria were not quite the same type as those from the Munich area. In 1938, when Philip Stockmann, who was the Boxer Breed Warden for Germany, came to America to judge a show, it was an ideal opportunity for him to meet representatives of the American Boxer Club, in the hope that the German Standard could be translated.

A meeting was arranged between Philip Stockmann, Jack Wagner, Enno Meyer – "an animal artist and judge" – and two German-speaking members of the ABC, who bred Boxers and had submitted a Standard from Austria to the ABC. After an all-night session, a translation of the current Munich Standard was adopted by the American Boxer Club. This has been slightly updated, but it is still largely based on the original translation of the Munich Standard. The greatest difference between the American and German Standards is that gait is not mentioned at all in the German version. The American Standard is reproduced here, with drawings by the artist Enno Meyer, who was at that historic meeting. The drawings and captions were later published in a book by Enno Meyer called *Judging The Boxer,* in 1951.

THE AMERICAN BREED STANDARD
(Revised 1989)

GENERAL APPEARANCE

The *ideal* Boxer is a medium-sized, square built dog of good substance with short back, strong limbs, and short, tight-fitting coat. His well-developed muscles are clean, hard and appear smooth under taut skin. His movements denote energy. The gait is firm, yet elastic, the stride free and ground-covering, the carriage proud. Developed to serve as guard, working and companion dog, he combines strength and agility with elegance and style. His expression is alert and temperament steadfast and tractable.

LINE DRAWINGS AND CAPTIONS BY ENNO MEYER

THE IDEAL MALE
Here we have the robust build indicative of the male, the distinct muscular development which, however, must not be exaggerated to such an extent as to mar the general smooth contour. Working dog structure demands that all component parts contribute to the exercise of required activities. The muzzle should be strong, but the skull not overdone since the active implements are in reality the powerful muscles which furnish motive power for the jaws, and these muscles should be fairly flat rather than bunchy. The strong neck must have sufficient length and suppleness, should fit into sloping shoulders, these into the well angulated upper arm, all synonymous with the correct front in a chest neither too wide nor too narrow. The front legs are parallel and of good bone; the pasterns are slightly sloping and the feet close.

The chiselled head imparts to the Boxer a unique individual stamp. It must be in correct proportion to the body. The broad, blunt muzzle is the distinctive feature, and great value is placed upon its being of proper form and balance with the skull.

In judging the Boxer, first consideration is given to general appearance to which attractive color and arresting style contribute. Next is overall balance with special attention devoted to the head, after which individual body components are examined for their correct construction, and efficiency of gait is evaluated.

THE
IDEAL
FEMALE

There is actually only a narrow margin of weight and height in properly balanced specimens of male and female, but the female must exhibit infinitely greater refinement by means of a smoother muscular development. In other words, the female, though not to be considered as lacking in strength, must have, above all else, the quality best described as femininity. While there is no provision for it in the standard, the female, on account of her maternal duties, should be allowed a slightly longer back than the male. Her back, however, is comparatively straight, with proper set-on of tail, the brisket reaching to the elbow, the body moderately tucked up, the hindquarters nicely angulated and the hocks strong. The legs are well boned but never clumsy.

BULLDOG TYPE
The Bulldog type of Boxer, sometimes met with, is heavy and overdone in its muscular system. It lacks the refinement which is typical of the breed in conjunction with its power, and it suggests some of the early types of dogs among its progenitors. While this illustration is somewhat overdrawn in this respect, it is done so purposely in order to enable the newcomer to recognize the type and to realize that the Boxer breed is already beyond many reversals to this type. However, if they do recur, we must remember that the Bulldog, after all, is one of the foundation stones upon which the Boxer is built; that we must retain a certain percentage of Bulldog essentials but, at the same time, not permit such characteristics to get beyond control.

TERRIER TYPE
As opposed to the Bulldog type of Boxer is the Terrier type of good, sound stance and conformation but lacking the muscular power and distinctive type of the correct specimen. While both types are incorrect, they are frequently useful as a foil, if a fixed tendency in either direction develops in a particular line of breeding, since dogs of this type are usually conspicuous for their short, straight backs, good shoulders, fronts, legs and feet, and sound gait. This illustration, too, is overdrawn, in the opposite direction to the Bulldog type, but it is done to emphasize in more easily understood fashion the mentioned opposing features. These very features are of importance to a breed which is not classed as a non-sporting dog but, instead, as a working dog.

GOOD BUT NOT A FLYER
Drawn from the same general, basic outline as our ideal male, this dog gives evidence of the right conformation, proportion and balance without any easily apparent fault, thus, seen by himself, he might be mistaken for a proper Boxer. A more minute inspection, though, will reveal no outstanding type. He lacks that style, finish and general flash which characterizes the real show star. Study him closely and you will call him a "pretty" Boxer. Compare him with our correct male and the great difference will at once become apparent.

Conspicuous by its absence is the sturdiness, the strength, the pronounced and beautiful musculature which contribute to the necessary quality of maleness and which, regardless of sex, spells the difference between a "pretty" dog and a true working dog.

OVER-ANGULATION
Here we have a dog of fair, over-all squareness but easily apparent faults, the most noticeable of which is over-angulation of the hindquarters. As a fault of conformation, this mars the general outline of the animal; more than that, it may impede the progress and staying power of the working dog not endowed by nature with a long, or fairly long, body. Couple with over-angulation the unfortunately flat feet shown in the illustration and we have two faults of mobility counting against the worker, as well as two faults of conformation

militating against the stance and gait of the dog in the show ring. To a lesser degree, the profusion of wrinkle, and the dewlap, both constitute undesirable features which detract from the Boxer's characteristic neatness.

THE SHELLY TYPE

This is truly a disagreeable type with little to commend it, a sort of dog which even at maturity seems undeveloped. The long, rather slack back appears longer still because of insufficient depth of brisket. The shallow chest cannot possibly provide enough room for hard-working heart and lungs, and that suggested weakness in loin and hindquarter must mean scant power for the drive of the rear assembly. The ribs themselves, in such a structure, are usually flat-sided, contributing markedly to the rangy nondescript body proper. The straight shoulder, too, militates against this dog whose forelegs seem to be pushed away from the body rather than molded onto it. Nor does the lack in muzzle help the general appearance.

STRAIGHT-STIFLED

The casual observer will have no trouble in spotting the faults of the dog portrayed in this illustration, for here are faults of a kind which come right out at you. No close study is needed to discern the poor quality, the atypical conformation and misfitting of the parts. The cloddy mold of the body has its usual accompaniment of pudginess and non-muscularity of loin, a condition frequently brought about by the straight stifle which cannot carry through real driving power. A stifle, straight to the point of exaggeration, coupled with a short back, can mean only one thing – a mincing gait, with

its inevitable up-and-down, as opposed to flowing motion, when the animal is on the run. The neck is so devoid of arch that the head appears stuck on, while the poorly cropped ears do not enhance the general appearance.

SIZE, PROPORTION, SUBSTANCE

Height: Adult males 22½ to 25 inches; females 21 to 23½ inches at the withers. Preferably, males should not be under the minimum nor females over the maximum; however, proper balance and quality in the individual should be of primary importance since there is no size disqualification.

Proportion: The body, in profile is of square proportion in that a horizontal line from the front of the forechest to the rear projection of the upper thigh should equal the length of a vertical line dropped from the top of the withers to the ground.

Substance: Sturdy with balanced musculature. Males larger boned than their female counterparts.

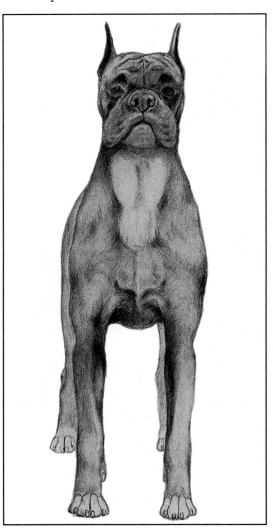

FRONT VIEW (Correct)
Viewed directly from the front, to greater degree perhaps than from any other vantage point, does a dog evidence characteristics of balance, particularly as regards those two balance-properties, station and substance. Here we find, first of all, the right proportion of over-all height to width. We see the right depth of chest as compared with width of chest; the right length of leg and comparative thickness and roundness of bone, from elbow to pastern to feet, with no suggestion of taper and equidistant throughout. The straight front, when accompanied by the correct slope of shoulder and the properly developed chest, is a thing of beauty which, in the presence of a well knit bony structure, spells admirable stance and commendable forepart gait.

FRONT VIEW (Incorrect)

Here we have two faulty builds, the one too narrow, the other too wide, both specimens typifying not faulty stance alone but, rather, the faulty structure responsible for faulty stance. In other words, no skilful setting down of feet and legs could serve to hide these true structural shortcomings. In the narrow fronted dog, the same unfortunate inheritance, or actual lack of bone growth which resulted in the undeveloped chest, produced also long bones of the legs which did not grow straight to stand equidistant from each other. Instead, they bowed, or knock-kneed, a deplorable malformation. The wide fronted dog, though his legs are straight and equidistant, is just as far from standard. He is so out of balance as to be chesty; he is wider in front that he is behind, thus wedge shaped, which a Boxer should not be.

HEAD

The beauty of the head depends upon harmonious proportion of muzzle to skull. The blunt muzzle is one-third the length of the head from the occiput to the tip of the nose, and two-thirds the width of the skull. The head should be clean, not showing deep wrinkles (wet). Wrinkles typically appear upon the forehead when ears are erect and folds are always present from the lower edge of the stop running downward on both sides of the muzzle.

Expression: Intelligent and alert.

Eyes: Dark brown in color, not too small, too protruding or too deepset. Their mood-mirroring character combined with the wrinkling of the forehead, gives the Boxer head its unique quality of expressiveness.

Ears: Set at the highest points of the sides of the skull are cropped, cut rather long and tapering, raised when alert.

Skull: The top of the skull is slightly arched, not rounded, flat nor noticeably broad, with the occiput not overly pronounced. The forehead shows a slight indentation between the eyes and forms a distinct stop with the topline of the muzzle. The cheeks should be relatively flat and not bulge (cheekiness), maintaining the clean lines of the skull, and should taper into the muzzle in a slight, graceful curve.

Muzzle: The muzzle, proportionately developed in length, width and depth, has a shape influenced first through the formation of both jawbones, second through the placement of the teeth, and third through the texture of the lips. The top of the muzzle should not slant down (downfaced), nor should it be concave (dish-faced): however, the tip of the nose should lie slightly higher than the foot of the muzzle.

The nose should be broad and black.

The upper jaw is broad where attached to the skull and maintains this breadth except for a very slight tapering to the front. The lips, which complete the formation of the muzzle, should meet evenly in front. The upper lip is thick and padded, filling out the frontal space created by the projection of the lower jaw, and laterally is supported by the canines of the lower jaw.

Therefore, these canines must stand far apart and be of good length so that the front surface of the muzzle is broad and squarish. Viewed from the side, the jaws show moderate layback. The chin should be perceptible from the side as well as from the front.

Bite: The Boxer bite is undershot; the lower jaw protrudes beyond the upper and curves slightly upward. The incisor teeth of the lower jaw are in a straight line, with the canines preferably up front in the same line to give the jaw the greatest possible width. The upper line of incisors is slightly convex with the corner upper incisors fitting snugly back of the lower canine teeth on each side.

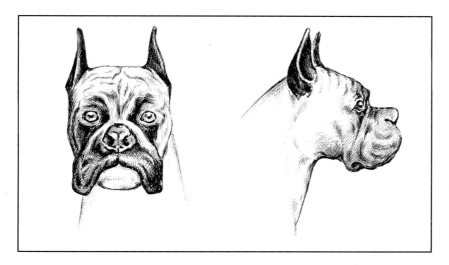

*Correct
Head*

The CORRECT Boxer head, as a whole appears muscular, for here lies the motive power for the jaws, yet it should in no way seem overdone. It is in balance when skull and foreface are in the right proportion. The skull is clean, the cheeks do not protrude, and there is no wrinkle save what may be occasioned by erection of the ears. In profile, the correct head shows relative length of skull and muzzle, the moderately rounded contour of the skull, the slight elevation of the nose and the proper depth of muzzle.

In creating the DANE-LIKE head, Nature, in an effort to produce a level mouth through elongation of the maxillary, premaxillary and mandible bones, shoves skull and muzzle down to maintain a natural balance. The result is a head whose long cast, and small eyes and nostrils constitute the antithesis of everything desired in a Boxer.

*Dane-like
Head*

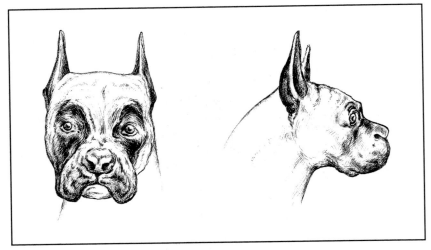

*Incorrect
proportion*

On account of its INCORRECT PROPORTION of skull and foreface, this head is faulty, for the size of the muzzle is too small as compared with the size of the skull. The head, therefore, appears weak; the muzzle naturally lacks power and, as a rule, possesses no vestige of turn-up. And the light eye, improperly set, gives the face an expression quite foreign to the Boxer. In profile, this head looks even weaker because of the downward slope of the muzzle.

In the BULLDOG TYPE of head, we have a reversion to one of the early progenitors of the breed – the flat Bulldog skull with profuse wrinkle, the stop receding into the skull with consequent abnormal shortening of the foreface. In profile, this head sometimes exhibits such marked turn-up as to expose the dentition of the lower jaw.

*Bulldog
type*

Correct neck

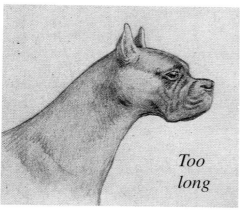

Too long

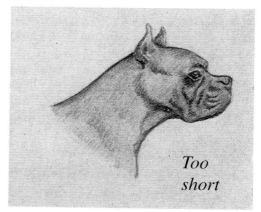

Too short

The neck is an important feature of the show dog's anatomy, contributing greatly to symmetry and balance. Of ample length, it must be strong and muscular and slightly arched at the nape. Yet it must be clean, dry and devoid of dewlap or pendulous skin under the throat. Such a neck joins head to body in a continuously graceful line. The TOO LONG neck projects the head away from the body, thus destroying balance. It appears stringy because it lacks roundedness and arch. The TOO SHORT neck is least graceful of all, being almost invariably thick, and too muscular. This neck, also, as a rule lacks arch while the dewlap, frequently observed in loose-skinned dogs, tends to make the head seem heavy and in that way to mar the harmony of the whole.

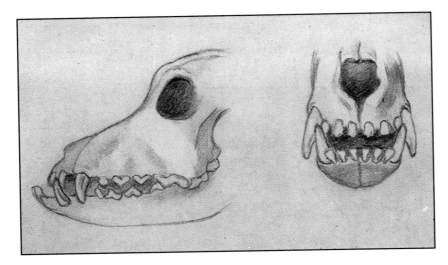

Correct bite

The dentition of the Boxer is an indicator of the correct construction and position of maxillary and premaxillary bones which constitute the upper jaw and the mandibles of the lower jaw. The correct bite consists of just enough protrusion of the lower jaw to merit the outer incisors of the upper jaw to pass behind the outer canines of the lower jaw. The front view discloses the desirable width of jaw together with even, regularly spaced incisors. In the diagram (lower left), we note too much length of underjaw leaving a gap between the upper incisor and the lower canine. Such a faulty mouth will, in it exaggerated form, show the teeth when the mouth is closed. The diagram (lower right), portrays what may be the perfect bite for some breeds but not for the Boxer, inasmuch, as it would so change the contour and character of the head as to suggest a terrier cast.

Incorrect bite

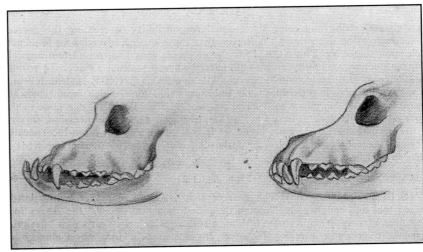

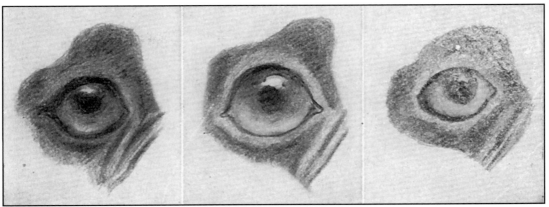

Normal   *Large, protruding*   *Small, deeply set*

Size, shape, setting and color share equal responsibility in creating the correct Boxer expression even though it is true that these qualities overlap in influence, each upon the other. The NORMAL Boxer eye is dark brown and luminous. It radiates energy, amiability and intelligence. It breathes trust as opposed to any semblance of craftiness or belligerence. The eye TOO LARGE is definitely not Boxer; ordinarily, it protrudes, and it has a vapid look which would indicate almost a lack of mental capacity. The SMALL, DEEPLY SET eye goes to the other extreme. If dark, it may have a threatening or piercing expression, foreign to the normal character of the breed. If it is light in color, it often incorporates a certain degree of shrewdness as if the dog must make up in cunning what it lacks in real brain power.

FAULTS: Skull too broad. Cheekiness. Wrinkling too deep (wet) or lacking (dry). Excessive flews. Muzzle too light for skull. Too pointed a bite (snipy), too undershot, teeth or tongue showing when mouth closed. Eyes noticeably lighter than ground color of coat.

NECK, TOPLINE, BODY
Neck: Round, of ample length, muscular and clean without excessive hanging skin (dewlap). The neck has a distinctly marked nape with an elegant arch blending smoothly into the withers.
Topline: Smooth, firm and slightly sloping.
Body: The chest is of fair width, and the forechest well defined and visible from the side. The brisket is deep, reaching down to the elbows; the depth of the body at the lowest point of the brisket equals half the height of the dog at the withers. The ribs, extending far to the rear, are well arched, but not barrel-shaped.

The back is short, straight and muscular and firmly connects the withers to the hindquarters.

The loins are short and muscular. The lower stomach line is lightly tucked up, blending into a graceful curve to the rear. The croup is slightly sloped, flat and broad. Tail is set high, docked and carried upward. Pelvis long and in females especially broad.

FAULTS: Short, heavy neck. Chest too broad, too narrow or hanging between shoulders. Lack of forechest. Hanging stomach. Slab-sided rib cage. Long or narrow loin, weak union with croup. Falling off of croup. Higher in rear than in front.

FOREQUARTERS

The shoulders are long and sloping, close-lying, and not excessively covered with muscle (loaded). The upper arm is long, approaching a right angle to the shoulder blade. The elbows should not press too closely to the chest wall nor stand off visibly from it.

The forelegs are long, straight and firmly muscled and when viewed from the front, stand parallel to each other. The pastern is strong and distinct, slightly slanting, but standing almost perpendicular to the ground. The dewclaws may be removed. Feet should be compact, turning neither in nor out, with well-arched toes.

FAULTS: Loose or loaded shoulders. Tied-in or bowed-out elbows.

HINDQUARTERS

The hindquarters are strongly muscled with angulation in balance with that of the forequarters.

The thighs are broad and curved, the breech musculature hard and strongly developed. Upper and lower thigh long. Leg well angulated at the stifle with a clearly defined, well "let down" hock joint. Viewed from behind, the hind legs should be straight with hock joints leaning neither in nor out. From the side, the leg below the hock (metatarsus) should be almost perpendicular to the ground, with a slight slope to the rear permissible. The metatarsus should be short, clean and strong. The Boxer has no rear dewclaws.

Faults: Steep or over-angulated hindquarters. Light thighs or over-developed hams. Over-angulated (sickle) hocks. Hindquarters too far under or too far behind.

COAT

Short, shiny, lying smooth and tight to the body.

COLOR

The colors are fawn and brindle. Fawn shades vary from light tan to mahogany. The brindle ranges from sparse, but clearly defined black stripes on a fawn background,

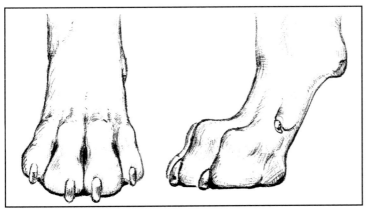

CORRECT FOOT: The correct foot is small, compact, with tightly arched toes and tough pads. Though described as a "cat's paw", the Boxer foot is as muscular as any other part of him, a feature which the "cat's paw" designation might seem to contradict. However, his is a graceful foot, never clumsy for all its strength. Viewed from the side, this foot is definitely square by virtue of its high-arched toes and strong ligaments.

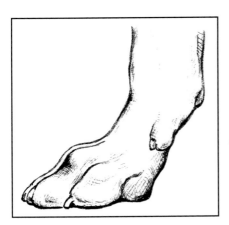

SPLAY FOOT: The open, or splay foot, is one whose toes are spread and flattened. Whether the condition is an hereditary malformation, or whether consequent upon calcium deficiency, the fact remains that it is a weak foot incapable of prolonged effort.

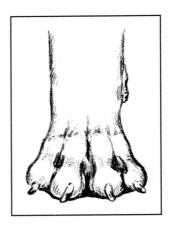

TURNED OUT FOOT: The turned out foot, too, is undesirable in that it mars stylish stance in the show room and militates against endurance when at work.

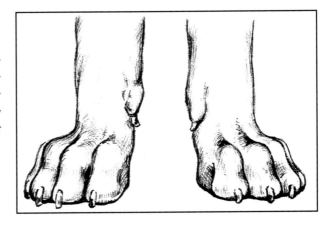

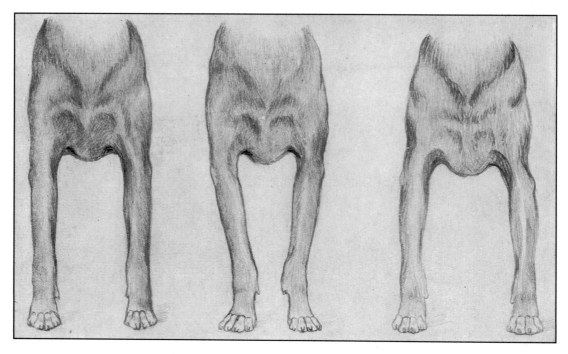

THE FRONT

In considering the front, we are concerned with more than legs and feet, bone and proportion, important as are these qualities in themselves. We are concerned, as well, with the legs as support for the body. Here we have three fronts, the one at the left correct with its straight, parallel forelegs, smooth, short pasterns and small, arched feet which together constitute sturdy underpinning for a powerful body. In the center view, the legs, in converging toward each other at the pasterns, can furnish only limited support, the appearance of weakness furthered by the narrow, undeveloped chest. To the right, we see another poor front caused primarily by shoulders so loose as to spread the front and thus rob the body of its rightful support.

to such a heavy concentration of black striping that the essential fawn background color barely, although clearly, shows through (which may create the appearance of "reverse brindling").

White markings should be of such distribution as to enhance the dog's appearance, but may not exceed one-third of the entire coat. They are not desirable on the flanks or on the back of the torso proper. On the face, white may replace part of the otherwise essential black mask and may extend in an upward path between the eyes, but it must not be excessive so as to detract from the true Boxer expression.
FAULTS: Unattractive or misplaced white markings.

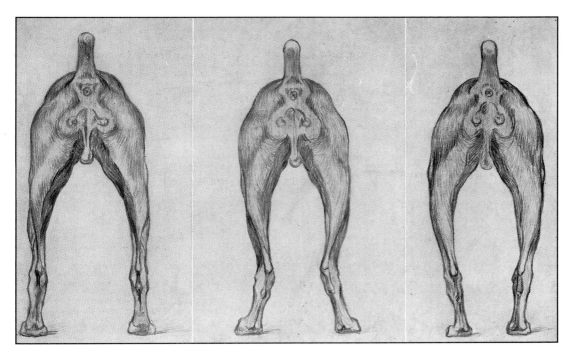

REAR VIEW

At the left, we have commendable stance as viewed from behind. The overall proportion of height to width is good, while the pronounced musculation must play its part in the grace and sturdiness of the natural stand. The pelvis is broad, the thighs long, the hocks well let down and the same distance from each other as are the feet. In the center view, the hocks turn in, bowing the quarters and forcing the feet to turn out, thus affecting not alone stability but starting momentum. To the right, we observe a second faulty formation in the outward bowing of the thigh bones, caused primarily by weakness at the stifle to create a disagreeable stance and what must prove to be a waddling gait.

DISQUALIFICATIONS: Boxers that are any color other than fawn or brindle. Boxers with a total of white markings exceeding one-third of the entire coat.

GAIT

Viewed from the side, proper front and rear angulation is manifested in a smoothly efficient, level-backed, ground-covering stride with powerful drive emanating from a freely operating rear. Although the front legs do not contribute impelling power, adequate "reach" should be evident to prevent interference, overlap or "sidewinding" (crabbing). Viewed from the front, the shoulders should remain trim

HINDQUARTER

The ideal hindquarter is first of all so strong that its muscles stand out through the skin; not bunchy, knotted or "muscled up," but seeming to flow with grace and rhythm even though the animal be absolutely still. For it is these muscles, in conjunction with the correct angulation of the bones, which furnish power for the drive and flexibility in motion. As here portrayed, it is the proportion of hip to hock, and hock to toe – roughly two thirds and one third – which means a sure and distance-eating

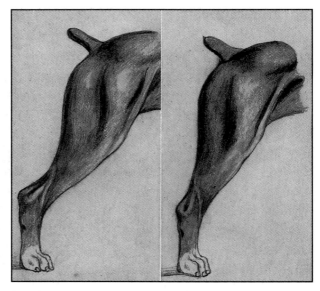

reach and a powerful and long enduring drive. Contrast this ideal hindquarter with the one at the right which is comparatively straight-stifled, neither graceful nor characteristic. The muscular development seems good, but the definite lack in angulation cannot provide for proper leverage to stretch and flex the muscles, thus it must produce a stilted gait.

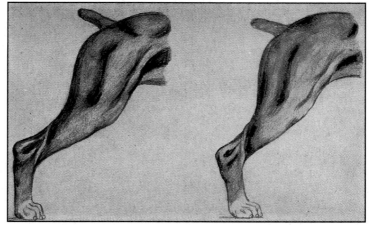

Exactly the reverse of the straight-stifled quarter is the over-angulation pictured at the left. The proportion of hock to toe is too great, and the quarter, as a sometime natural consequence, is stringy. There must be lost motion here, for muscles cannot deliver when impeded by such faulty angulation. The gait is almost sure to be loose, shifty, uncertain, and the effort entailed in producing it, extremely tiring. To the right, we see a hindquarter which appears really satisfactory in its muscularity, though markedly at fault through the set-under position of the hock. Such a build interferes with the propulsion of the entire hindquarter, the lack of power being evident even in the slack setting down of the foot.

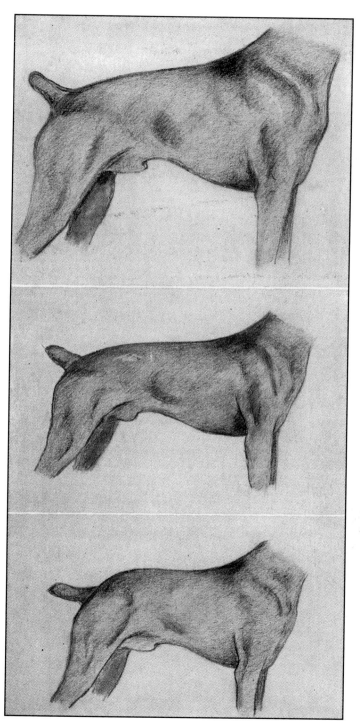

THE BODY

Correct

The correct body impresses one first of all with its squareness, and then with its characteristic backline which, starting from the high point at the withers, comes down in a graceful but very slight curve across the back and on over the croup to the set-on of the tail. The deep chest reaches to the elbows, the well sprung ribs shorten as they approach the loin to produce a moderate tuck-up.

Long Back

Here we note the plain effect produced by the over-long back and the straight shoulder, this build often being accompanied by scant depth of brisket and a general deficiency in substance.

Slanting Croup

This model is conspicuous for its thoroughly atypical backline, its croup, or rump, being too markedly slanting and its tail set low.

CARP BACK

There are two extremely faulty formations which, though not often encountered in the show room, should be given space if for no other reason than to serve as a warning of what to avoid. In what is usually known as the CARP BACK, the backline is so convex as to dip at the withers and again at the tail. The general appearance produced is a hunching of the body, the antithesis of true Boxer mould, and it is often accompanied by the straight shoulder, improperly knit. The SWAY BACK is just as undesirable though it may spell weakness in even greater degree because it is part and parcel of undeveloped, straight-sided ribs and weediness throughout. In such specimens, the rump is usually over-built and the total ensemble that of an unsightly misfit.

SWAY BACK

and the elbows not flare out. The legs are parallel until gaiting narrows the track in proportion to increasing speed, then the legs come in under the body but should never cross. The line from the shoulder down through the leg should remain straight although not necessarily perpendicular to the ground. Viewed from the rear, a Boxer's rump should not roll. The hind feet should "dig in" and track relatively true with the front. Again, as speed increases, the normally broad rear track will become narrower.

FAULTS: Stilted or inefficient gait. Lack of smoothness.

CHARACTER AND TEMPERAMENT

These are of paramount importance in the Boxer. Instinctively a "hearing" guard dog, his bearing is alert, dignified and self-assured. In the show ring, his behaviour should exhibit constrained animation. With family and friends, his temperament is fundamentally playful, yet patient and stoical with children. Deliberate and wary with strangers, he will exhibit curiosity, but, most importantly, fearless courage if threatened. However, he responds promptly to friendly overtures honestly rendered. His intelligence, loyal affection and tractability to discipline make him a highly desirable companion.

FAULTS: Lack of dignity and alertness. Shyness.

DISQUALIFICATIONS

Boxers that are any color other than fawn or brindle. Boxers with a total of white markings exceeding one-third of the entire coat.

Reproduced by kind permission of the American Kennel Club (1989).

Across the Atlantic, in the 1930s, the newly-formed British Boxer Dog Club Committee was struggling with the preparation of a Standard. Allon Dawson, a committee member, produced an excellent version illustrated by photographs, including many of the von Dom Boxers. There were several committee meetings to discuss the Standard, and Allon Dawson admitted that "the committee members were novices as far as drawing up a Standard was concerned." Many of the members had barely three years experience of Boxers, and so had their own erroneous ideas of how the Breed should be. At about this time, the ABC's translation of the Munich Standard was sent over for the British Boxer Dog Club to discuss, and because of the involvement of Philip Stockmann in the translation, it was adopted by the British Boxer Dog Club. Unfortunately, copies of this Standard were not circulated to members straightaway, and with the outbreak of the Second World War, the British Boxer Dog Club was suspended for the duration.

As far as I can gather, there was no official written Boxer Standard for the few Boxer enthusiasts during the War. This was a desperate situation for a new breed – no wonder they were clamouring for information, and poring over the few available copies of Jack Wagner's new book, *The Boxer*. In 1943 the ABC Standard was serialised weekly in *Dog World* Boxer Breed Notes by Kitty Guthrie. This caused much interest, arguments and correspondence. As soon as the war ended, the newly named British Boxer Club submitted the American version of the German Standard to the Kennel Club; the only difference was in the 'Ears', as cropping is banned by law in the UK. The Kennel Club approved the Standard as submitted, and all of us breeders and judges were quite satisfied and worked well with the Kennel Club Standard. With decimalisation, heights and weights had to be altered to conform with the German Standard. In the 1980s, the Kennel Club decided to 'unify' all Breed Standards to make them easier to read and understand, and the Boxer Breed Council were asked by the KC to undertake this project. All the Boxer Clubs affiliated to the Breed Council were already perfectly satisfied with Kennel Club Standard, and they said so. However, they were still asked to submit a 'unified' Standard, modified for the Kennel Club's approval. All Boxer Clubs designated a member for a sub-committee to review and unify the Standard. I was selected for this job, along with Pat Withers, Joan McLaren, Bill Malcolm, Barbara Murray, Ivor Ward-Davis and David Spencer, and we were joined by Ann Podmore, the secretary of the Breed Council, who was to take notes.

This Standard Sub-Committee, which was rapidly renamed the 'Sub Standard Committee', met frequently, but rather reluctantly, throughout most of the year, trying to reach an agreement before the Kennel Club's deadline. The task was far from easy. The Kennel Club's desire for a shorter, less wordy Standard meant that every word had to be carefully chosen if the new Standard was to give as precise a picture of the Boxer as its predecessor. When the deadline was passed, a meeting was held with the Kennel Club Standard Committee, which was to agree the new approved Standards of all breeds, and our views and opinions were discussed and listened to, and, in some cases, were included in the new approved Kennel Club Boxer Standard.

The Boxer Breed Council have issued a little booklet which is available to all Boxer Club members, and is entitled *Blueprint of the Boxer*. This contains the 'blueprint', which takes up five pages of the booklet. The Kennel Club Approved Standard of the Boxer is a meagre one and a half pages in length. I wonder what those early pioneers would think if they were alive today, seeing the Standard of their 'superbreed', which has been handed down to us for safe-keeping through generations (on both sides of the Atlantic), reduced to just one and a half pages!

BLUEPRINT OF THE BOXER

CHARACTERISTICS

The character of the Boxer is of the greatest importance and demands the most careful attention. He is renowned from olden times for his great love and faithfulness to his master and household, his alertness and fearless courage as a defender and protector. The Boxer is docile but distrustful of strangers. He is bright and friendly in play but brave and determined when roused. His intelligence and willing tractability, his modesty and cleanliness make him a highly desirable family dog and cheerful companion. He is the soul of honesty and loyalty. He is never false or treacherous even in his old age.

GENERAL APPEARANCE

The Boxer is a medium sized, sturdy, smooth-haired dog of short, square figure and strong limb. The musculation is clean and powerfully developed, and should stand out plastically from under the skin. Movement of the Boxer should be alive with energy. His gait, although firm, is elastic. The stride free and roomy; carriage proud and noble. As a service and guard dog he must combine a considerable degree of elegance with the substance and power essential to his duties; those of an enduring escort dog whether with horse, bicycle or carriage and as a splendid jumper. Only a body whose individual limbs are built to withstand the most strenuous "mechanical" effort and assembled as a complete and harmonious whole, can respond to such demands. Therefore, to be at its highest efficiency, the Boxer must never be plump or heavy. Whilst equipped for great speed, it must not be racy. When judging the Boxer, the first thing to be considered is general appearance, the relation of substance to elegance and the desired relationship of the individual parts of the body to each other. Consideration, too, must be given to colour. After these, the individual parts should be examined for their correct construction and their functions. Special attention should be devoted to the head.

HEAD AND SKULL

The head imparts to the Boxer a unique individual stamp peculiar to the breed. It must be in perfect proportion to his body; above all it must never be too light. The muzzle is the most distinctive feature. The greatest value is to be placed on its being of correct form and in absolute proportion to the skull. The beauty of the head depends upon the harmonious proportion between the muzzle and the skull. From whatever direction the head is viewed, whether from the front, from the top or from the side, the muzzle should always appear in correct relationship to the skull. That

Ch. Biloran Mr Similarity: A highly successful show dog, praised for his typical Boxer head. Winner of seven CCs and three Reserve CCs.

Pearce.

Biloran Doctor Wosky: A son of Ch. Biloran Mr Similarity.

Pearce.

means that the head should never appear too small or too large. The length of the muzzle to the whole of the head should be as 1 is to 3.

The head should not show deep wrinkles. Normally wrinkles will spring up on the top of the skull when the dog is alert. Folds are always indicated from the root of the nose running downwards on both sides of the muzzle. The dark mask is confined to the muzzle. It must be in distinct relief to the colour of the head so that the face will not have a "sombre" expression. The muzzle must be powerfully developed in length, in breadth and in height. It must not be pointed or narrow; short or shallow. Its shape is influenced through the formation of both jaw-bones, the placement of teeth in the jaw-bones, and through the quality of the lips.

The top of the skull should be slightly arched. It should not be so short that it is rotund, too flat, or too broad. The occiput should not be too pronounced. The forehead should form a distinct stop with the top line of the muzzle, which should not be forced back into the forehead like that of a Bulldog. Neither should it slope away (downfaced). The tip of the nose should lie somewhat higher than the root of the muzzle. The forehead should show a suggestion of furrow which, however, should never be too deep, especially between the eyes.

Corresponding with the powerful set of teeth, the cheeks accordingly, should be well developed without protruding from the head with "too bulgy" an appearance. For preference they should taper into the muzzle in a slight, graceful curve. The nose should be broad and black, very slightly turned up. The nostrils should be broad with a naso-labial line between them. The two jaw-bones should not terminate in a normal perpendicular level in the front but the lower jaw should protrude beyond the upper jaw and bend slightly upwards. The Boxer is normally undershot. The upper jaw should be broad where attached to the skull, and maintain this breadth except for a very slight tapering to the front.

EYES

The eyes should be dark brown; not too small or protruding; not deep set. They should disclose an expression of energy and intelligence, but should never appear gloomy, threatening or piercing. The eyes must have a dark rim.

EARS

Some American and Continental Boxers are cropped and are ineligible for competition under Kennel Club Regulations. The Boxer's natural ears are defined as: moderate in size (small rather than large), thin to the touch, set on wide apart at the highest points of the sides of the skull and lying flat and close to the cheek when in repose. When the dog is alert the ears should fall forward with a definite crease.

MOUTH
The canine teeth should be as widely separated as possible. The incisors (6) should all be in one row, with no projection of the middle teeth. In the upper jaw they should be slightly concave. In the lower they should be in a straight line. Both jaws should be very wide in front; bite powerful and sound, the teeth set in the most normal possible arrangement. The lips complete under the formation of the muzzle. The upper lip should be thick and padded and fill out the hollow space in front formed by the projection of the lower jaw and be supported by the fangs of the jaw.

These fangs must stand as far apart as possible and be of good length so that the front surface of the muzzle becomes broad and almost square, to form an obtuse (rounded) angle with the top line of the muzzle. The lower edge of the upper lip should rest on the edge of the lower lip. The repandous (bent upward) part of the under-jaw with the lower lip (sometimes called the chin) must not rise above the front of the upper lip. On the other hand, it should not disappear under it. It must, however, be plainly perceptible when viewed from the front as well as from the side, without protruding and bending upward as in the English Bulldog. The teeth of the under-jaw should not be seen when the mouth is closed, neither should the tongue show when the mouth is closed.

NECK
The neck should not be too thick and short but of ample length, yet strong, round, muscular and clean-cut throughout. There should be a distinctly marked nape and an elegant arch down to the back.

FOREQUARTERS
The chest should be deep and reach down to the elbows. The depth of the chest should be half the height of the dog at the withers. The ribs should be well arched but not barrel-shaped. They should extend far to the rear. The loins should be short, close and taut and slightly tucked up. The lower stomach line should blend into an elegant curve to the rear. The shoulders should be long and sloping, close lying but not excessively covered with muscle. The upper arm should be long and form a right-angle to the shoulder blade.

The forelegs when seen from the front should be straight, parallel to each other and have strong, firmly articulated (joined) bones. The elbows should not press too closely to the chest-wall or stand off too far from it. The underarm should be perpendicular, long, and firmly muscled. The pastern joint of the foreleg should be clearly defined, but not distended. The pastern should be short, slightly slanting and almost perpendicular to the ground.

BODY

The body viewed in profile should be of square appearance. The length of the body from the front of the chest to the rear of the body should equal the height from the ground to the top of the shoulder, giving the Boxer a short-coupled, square profile. The torso rests on trunk-like straight legs with strong bones. The withers should be clearly defined. The whole back should be short, straight, broad and very muscular.

HINDQUARTERS

The hindquarters should be strongly muscled. The musculation should be hard and stand out plastically through the skin. The thighs should not be narrow and flat but broad and curved. The breech musculation should also be strongly developed. The croup should be slightly sloped, flat, arched and broad. The pelvis should be long, and in females especially, broad. The upper and lower thighs should be long. The hip and knee joints should have as much angle as possible. In a standing position the knee should reach so far forward that it would meet a vertical line drawn from the hip protuberance to the floor. The hock angle should be about 140 degrees; the lower part of the foot at a slight slope of about 95 to 100 degrees from the hock joint to the floor; that is, not completely vertical. Seen from behind, the hind legs should be straight. The hocks should be clean and not distended, supported by powerful rear pads. Male animals should have two apparently normal testicles fully descended into the scrotum.

FEET

The feet should be small with tightly-arched toes (cat feet) and hard soles. The rear toes should be just a little longer than the front toes, but similar in all other respects.

TAIL

The tail attachment should be high. The tail should be docked and carried upwards and should not be more than 2 inches long.

COAT

The coat should be short and shiny, lying smooth and tight to the body.

COLOUR

The permissible colours are fawn, brindle and fawn in various shades from light yellow to dark deer red. The brindle variety should have black stripes on a golden-yellow or red-brown background. The stripes should be clearly defined and above all should not be grey or dirty. Stripes that do not cover the whole top of the body are not desirable. White markings are not undesirable; in fact they are often very attractive in appearance. The black mask is essential, but when white stretches over the muzzle, naturally that portion of the black mask disappears. It is not possible to get black toe-nails with white feet. It is desirable, however, to have an even distribution of head markings.

WEIGHT AND SIZE
Dogs: 22 to 24 inches at the withers. Bitches: 21 to 23 inches at the withers. Heights above or below these figures not to be encouraged. Dogs around 23 inches should weigh about 66 lb and bitches of about 22 inches should weigh about 62 lb.

FAULTS
Viciousness; treachery; unreliability; lack of temperament; cowardice; Head: a head that is not typical. A plump, bulldoggy appearance. Light bone. Lack of proportion. Bad physical condition. Lack of nobility and expression. "Sombre" face. Unserviceable bite whether due to disease or to faulty tooth placement. Pinscher or Bulldog head. Showing the teeth or the tongue. A sloping top line of the muzzle. Too pointed or too light a bite (snipy). Eyes: visible conjunctive (Haw). Light eyes. Ears: flying ears; rose ears; semi-erect or erect ears. Neck: dewlap. Front: too broad and low in front; loose shoulders; chest hanging between the shoulders; hare feet; turned legs and toes. Body: carp (roach) back; sway back thin, lean back; long narrow, sharp-sunken-in loins. Weak union with the croup, hollow flanks; hanging stomach. Hindquarters: a falling off or too arched or narrow croup. A low-set tail; higher in the back than in front; steep, stiff or too little angulation of the hindquarters; light thighs; cow-hocks; bow legs; hind dewclaws; soft hocks, narrow heel, tottering, waddling gait; hare's feet; hindquarters too far under or too far behind. Colour: Boxers with white or black ground colour, or entirely white or black or any other colour than fawn or brindle. (White markings are allowed but must not exceed one-third of the ground colour.)
Reproduced by kind permission of the Boxer Breed Council.

THE ENGLISH BREED STANDARD (1988)

GENERAL APPEARANCE Great nobility, smooth-coated, medium-sized, square build, strong bone and evident, well developed muscles.

CHARACTERISTICS Lively, strong, loyal to owner and family, but distrustful of strangers. Obedient, friendly at play, but with guarding instinct.

TEMPERAMENT Equable, biddable, fearless, self-assured.

HEAD AND SKULL Head imparts its unique individual stamp and is in proportion to body, appearing neither light nor too heavy. Skull lean, without exaggerated cheek muscles. Muzzle broad, deep and powerful, never narrow, pointed, short or shallow. Balance of skull and muzzle essential, with muzzle never appearing small, viewed from any angle. Skull cleanly covered, showing no wrinkle, except when alerted. Creases present from root of nose running down sides of muzzle. Dark mask confined to muzzle, distinctly contrasting with colour of head, even when white is present. Lower jaw undershot, curving slightly upward. Upper jaw broad where attached to skull, tapering very slightly to front. Muzzle shape completed by upper lips, thick and well padded, supported by well separated canine teeth of lower jaw. Lower edge of upper lip rests on edge of lower lip, so that chin is clearly perceptible when viewed from front or side. Lower jaw never to obscure front of upper lip, neither should teeth nor tongue be visible when mouth closed. Top of skull slightly arched, not rounded, nor too flat and broad. Occiput not too pronounced. Distinct stop, bridge of nose never forced back into forehead, nor should it be downfaced. Length of muzzle measured from tip of nose to inside corner of eye is one third length of head measured from tip of nose to occiput. Nose broad, black, slightly turned up, wide nostrils with well defined line between. Tip of nose set slightly higher than root of muzzle. Cheeks powerfully developed, never bulging.

EYES Dark brown, forward looking, not too small, protruding or deeply set. Showing lively intelligent expression. Dark rims with good pigmentation showing no haw.

EARS Moderate size, thin, set wide apart on highest part of skull lying flat and close to cheek in repose, but falling forward with definite crease when alert.

MOUTH Undershot jaw, canines set wide apart with incisors (six) in straight line in lower jaw. In upper jaw set in line curving slightly forward. Bite powerful and sound, with teeth set in normal arrangement.

NECK Round, of ample length, strong, muscular, clean cut, no dewlap. Distinctly marked nape and elegant arch down to withers.

FOREQUARTERS Shoulders long and sloping, close lying, not excessively covered with muscle. Upper arm long, making right angle to shoulder blade. Forelegs seen from front, straight, parallel, with strong bone. Elbows not too close or standing too far from chest wall. Forearms perpendicular, long and firmly muscled. Pasterns short, clearly defined but not distended, slightly slanted.

BODY In profile square, length from forechest to rear of upper thigh equal to height of withers. Chest deep, reaching to elbows. Depth of chest half height at withers. Ribs well arched, not barrel shaped, extending well to rear. Withers clearly defined. Back short, straight, slightly sloping, broad and strongly muscled. Loin short, well tucked up and taut. Lower abdominal line blends into curve to rear.

HINDQUARTERS Very strong with muscles hard and standing out noticeably under skin. Thighs broad and curved. Broad croup slightly sloped, with flat, broad arch. Pelvis long and broad. Upper and lower thigh long. Good hind angulation, when standing, the stifle is directly under the hip protuberance. Seen from side, leg from hock joint to foot not quite vertical. Seen from behind, legs straight, hock joints clean, with powerful rear pads.

FEET Front feet small and cat-like, with well arched toes, and hard pads; hind feet slightly longer.

TAIL Set on high, customarily docked and carried upward.

GAIT/MOVEMENT Strong, powerful with noble bearing, reaching well forward and with driving action of hindquarters. In profile, stride free and ground covering.

COAT Short, glossy, smooth and tight to body.

COLOUR Fawn or brindle. White markings acceptable not exceeding one third of ground colour.
Fawn : Various shades from dark deer red to light fawn.
Brindle: Black stripes on previously described fawn shades, running parallel to ribs all over body. Stripes contrast distinctly to ground colour, neither too close not too thinly dispersed. Ground colour clear not intermingling with stripes.

SIZE Height: Dogs 57-63 cm ($22_{1/2}$-25 in); Bitches: 53-59 cm (21-23 in). Weight: Dogs approximately 30-32 kg (66-70 lb); Bitches approximately 25-27 kg (55-60 lb).

FAULTS Any departure from the foregoing points should be considered a fault and the seriousness with which the fault should be regarded should be in exact proportion to its degree.

NOTE Male animals should have two apparently normal testicles fully descended into the scrotum.
Reproduced by kind permission of the English Kennel Club.

SUMMARY

All four Standards reproduced are based on the original, approved by the Munich Boxer Club in 1905. This Munich Club became the German Boxer Club and in all matters pertaining to the Boxer over-rules the German Kennel Club (Federation Cynologique Internationale).

TYPE

When I was in America at the American Boxer Club Specialty I was very impressed with the uniformity of type. This was far more marked than in the UK, and it is interesting to speculate as to how breeders in such a large country have achieved this. In fact, although both the American and British Breeds Standards are based on the original Standard drawn up in Munich, there are now major differences in type between the UK, the Continent and America.

Breeders in America have developed a beautiful Boxer, with extremely clean lines. The emphasis is on elegance rather than substance; the American Boxer is not a rugged dog. In the UK the Boxer is of varying type. It is more like the type of Boxer seen on the Continent, although not quite so rugged and out-going. Sometimes, when I have been at a show on the Continent I have seen a Boxer that has simply taken my breath away – it has been so impressive to look at. This is the Boxer at its best, and it is something that all breeders should strive to attain.

MOVEMENT

I think it is interesting that the German (FCI) Standard has no mention of movement or gait. We have a marvellous description of a magnificent Boxer, in profile, standing still, looking noble, who "is an escort dog with lively temperament, who must not have a tottering or waddling gait". It was in the English Standard taken from the early American one, mulled over in the small hours in 1938, by Philip Stockmann and members of the ABC, that the Boxer became "an escort with horse, bicycle and carriage and a splendid jumper".

This is strange, as on the Continent at shows, either Boxer Club Championship

*Am. Can. Ch. Woos
End Million Heir,
bred by Jack
Billhandt.*

*Jacquet's Cambridge Fortune, bred
by William Dunn and Richard
Tomita, owned in partnership with
Ikoko Ohtani, handled by Marylou
Hatfield. 'Casey' is the 115th AKC
Champion bred by the Jacquet
Boxers, and she is currently the top-
winning bitch in the USA.*

Ch. Hi-Techs Arbitrage, bred by Dr and Mrs William Trusedale and handled by Kim Pastella. 'Biff' was the winner of the 1992 ABC Top Twenty competition, and is a multiple Best of Breed, Working Group and Best in Show winner.

Ch. Kiebla's Tradition of Turo, bred by Kitty Barker, owned by Bruce and Jeannie Korson and handled by Christine Baum. 'Tiggin' has won 47 Best in Shows, over 50 Boxer Specialties, winner of the Working Group at the 1991 Westminster KC Show, and winner of Best of Breed at the ABC National in 1991, 1992 and 1993.

Swed. Ch. Impressives Naughty But Nice: A Boxer with an undocked tail who has been highly successful in the show ring.

Shows or Boxer classes at General Championship Shows, a great deal of attention is paid to movement and gait. Very often a judge will select his six or seven potential winners in a class, then ask these to move round and round the ring in an extended trot over and over again. Those who flag after a while and develop a "rolling" gait (wobbling from side to side) are dismissed in turn; the dogs who can continue to trot fast and steadily are then placed, probably first and second.

In the UK we seem to be more concerned with how our Boxers move more slowly for a short distance: how it uses its legs, and where it puts its feet, than if it is able to endure a long journey "with horse, bicycle, or carriage". On the Continent, a Boxer is thought of and called a "galloping breed".

DOCKING
This is a highly controversial area, and there are now a number of countries that ban docking. In the UK, this operation must now be carried out by a vet, rather than the breeder, and there are now moves to ban docking altogether. Obviously, this poses major problems for the Boxer breed, and it is impossible to foresee what effect this will have on the overall appearance of the Boxer.

Chapter Ten

THE SHOW RING

If you want to broaden the enjoyment of owning a Boxer, you can take part in competitions, dog shows or obedience shows. Dog shows are like beauty competitions for dogs, while obedience shows are competitions to show how obedient your dog is with you as pilot. There are several grades of these competitions, and these are advertised each week in the canine press.

It is a good idea to start off by going in for an informal competition, such as a match, to see if you, and your dog, enjoy competing. Matches are usually organised on the knock-out basis, two dogs meet, and the one who wins goes into the next round until there is an overall winner. There may be classes for dogs of differing ages and experience and it is quite a good training ground. You can then graduate to bigger events.

UK SHOWS
SANCTION SHOWS AND LIMITED SHOWS: These are run by clubs, sometimes Breed Clubs, and are limited to club members, so, at least, you only meet dogs of the same breed. You will be able to compare your Boxer with the other Boxers and learn to know the quality of your Boxer.

OPEN SHOWS: These are open to all, whether members of a club or not. All Breed Open Shows may not have classes for Boxers. If Boxers are to be judged, you find out who is judging in the canine press. The schedule, which can be obtained from the secretary of the club, will tell you the number of classes allocated for the breed. No dog can be shown until it is six months old. Some classes are for puppies, others for more experienced animals who have been shown, not always according to age.

These Open Shows, particularly Boxer Club Shows, are probably the best way to start the show career of your puppy, for at these shows you can meet many Boxer Breeders. The classes are divided by sex, into dog and bitch classes, and by age as well as previous wins. If you and your Boxer do well at a Club Open Show, it might be worth going to the top grade of dog shows, a Championship Show.

CHAMPIONSHIP SHOWS: There are about thirty Championship Shows where Boxers are scheduled during the year, from Northern Ireland, Scotland and throughout England, as far south as Paignton. Boxers entered at these shows are usually numerous, from well over 100 to as many as 300 at some shows. Classes are divided between dogs and bitches, the dog classes are always judged first. There may be a minor puppy class, which is only for pups between six and nine months of age, and these sometimes have over fifty puppies competing.

A puppy class is for pups up to one year old, and, in my opinion, this is quite early enough for many Boxers, but that is up to you. Other classes are age-related, or graded on previous show wins for each dog, eventually culminating in the Open Classes, which any dog can enter and which usually contain several Champions. At the end of the classes, there is the Challenge, where the winners of each class compete for the Challenge Certificate, which goes to the best, in the judge's opinion, dog or bitch at that show.

Three of these Challenge Certificates have to be won by a dog or bitch before that Boxer can be called a Champion – and you have to have a really outstanding Boxer to achieve that accolade. The top places are awarded based on the personal opinion of a judge, who, in all cases, should be judging to the Boxer Standard and not on a comparison between the other Boxers in the class. However, everyone who interprets the Boxer Standard, interprets it in a slightly different manner, and that is why the same dogs do not win all the time.

AMERICAN SHOWS

MATCHES
The local All Breed and Specialty Clubs will probably hold one or two Matches a year. These are advertised in the canine press, giving details of breeds, classes and judges. Entries are made on the morning of the show. They are often used as a training ground for people who are aspiring to judge at Championship show level. Classes usually range from Puppy through Novice to Open. Champions are not eligible to compete in Matches.

CHAMPIONSHIP SHOWS
These can be All Breed, Group or Breed shows. They are advertised in the canine press, and premiums are sent to all intending exhibitors. After the closing date for

entires, passes, catalog numbers and schedules are sent to exhibitors. Points are awarded towards the Championship title by a judge who is approved by the Kennel Club. A total of fifteen points under three different judges must be gained for a dog to become a Champion, including two 'majors' under separate judges (3, 4, or 5 point wins).

SPECIALTIES

These are held annually or bi-annually by the club concerned, usually attracting large entries. Again, Championship points are awarded. The judge is normally someone held in high esteem by breeders and exhibitors, and sometimes an overseas judge receives an invitation to judge.

JUDGING

Most countries have their own rules for dog shows and judging. At some Boxer Club shows in America, the entries can be very numerous. Fewer classes are scheduled than in the UK, and the colours, fawns and brindles, are judged separately, as they are on the Continent. The dogs in America are presented beautifully, mainly by professional handlers, who make sure that the dogs are very well trained and the handler makes the best of a dog's good points, and disguises the faults. I do have to say that the rapport between Boxer and handler is wonderful to see; the dogs obviously love the handler and you must love dogs to become a handler.

I went to America to see the 1993 American Boxer Club Specialty at Newark, New Jersey, and this proved to be a real Boxer bonanza with over 1,000 breed fanciers taking over the Holiday Inn for a week. One of the highspots was a competition for the top twenty Boxers of the United States. This was a real spectacle, with each dog parading under the spotlight for three judges – Mrs Leathers Billings, Mrs Shirley de Boer and Mrs Linda Huffman, all in full evening dress, as were the stewards, officials and many of the handlers. This was certainly a new angle on dog showing, especially for those of us from the UK.

In Australia, there is far more discipline in the show ring. Exhibitors collect their ring numbers outside the ring from a steward; when all the exhibitors are together, a gate into the ring is opened, and exhibitor and dog go into the ring in numerical order. After the last exhibitor, the gate is closed and no-one else is allowed to enter. The dogs and exhibitors stand in the ring in the same order and the judge goes over them in that order. The Boxers are extremely well show trained, topped and tailed, and have also been trained to move at a steady speed; I was told that walking machines are often used. Judging Boxers over there is certainly a pleasure.

In all continental countries, a completely different attitude is taken to dog shows.

These are far more relaxed. Most of the dogs come into the ring at the start of the class, standing around, handler and dog, the dog probably barking at his neighbour, or at a dog he knows across the ring. Each dog is called into the centre and at this time the other dogs seem to fade away; so a very careful assessment of the dog in the centre of the ring is made, and typed at the same time by a ring secretary.

A great deal of time is spent on the mouth and teeth, and the dog has usually been taught to sit down, while the owner or handler opens its mouth. A short move is asked for; it is only after the last few Boxers have been pulled out, that movement at length is wanted. The last few dogs are then moved round and round the ring to see which one holds out for the longest time. Quite often, spare handlers will take over a dog at the run.

THE JUDGE'S ROLE

Everyone seems to want to jump on the bandwagon and become a judge. However, I feel that you should have been going to dog shows for at least ten years before you undertake a judging appointment. You must be quite sure in your own mind that you can look at all Boxers with a completely detached eye, and you must be able to compare every Boxer with the Boxer Standard, and not to the other Boxers in the ring. Judging should be looked upon as an intellectual exercise. It is certainly an examination you have to undertake in public, with your peers to judge you. There are Breed Council Judging Lists, for most grades of judges, and the criteria of these lists should be followed.

Make sure if you have a judging appointment, that you arrive in time, and have a pencil and notebook or a hand-held mobile recorder, so that you can report on the dogs. You should dress neatly and have comfortable shoes – you have a lot of walking to do when judging a dog show. Remember that the ringside audience will see your back view for most of the time; the dogs will change in each class, but you and your back view will be there all the time!

Do not to look too fierce, although you must not show your feelings if one dog pleases you more than another, and try to say something pleasant to everybody – dogs and humans. When going over the dogs, follow the same routine for every dog. Always look at each dog all the time when it is moving; I do not like all the dogs to go round the ring at the same time – it makes me giddy. Always place the dogs in the same way, in the same part of the ring, and then you keep track of all the entries. Everyone learns by experience, and if this is a side of the dog world that appeals to you, I wish you the best of luck!

Chapter Eleven

BREEDING BOXERS

Before deciding to breed from your Boxer bitch, as well as considering personal and family commitments, decisions have also to be taken about the bitch herself, and enquiries made, pedigrees studied, advice asked for and given. So do not rush into anything, take it easy! Your bitch must be of good quality, and you must have the space and the time to devote to the resulting pups for at least ten weeks. Too many unwanted puppies are born, ending up in rescue units, and so you should think long and hard before you embark on producing more puppies. The next step is to to make sure that there are no reasons which should bar your bitch from having healthy puppies. Begin with a visit to your vet with the bitch, whom he may know well.

HEREDITARY CONDITIONS
When your vet has passed your bitch fit and well, it is time for you to do your homework. Three hereditary problems immediately come to mind: Progressive Axonopathy (PA), Hip Dysplasia (HD) and some heart conditions.

PROGRESSIVE AXONOPATHY: This is a disease affecting the nervous system. Although similar diseases are found in other breeds of dogs and other animals, this particular disease is found only in Boxers. PA is a hereditary disease, the mode of inheritance being that of a simple recessive gene, like that for white puppies.

In the UK there is an advisory leaflet which can be obtained from the secretary of your local Boxer Breed Club. This leaflet gives a list of carriers and a list of cleared dogs. Read these lists carefully, making sure that there are no carriers in either the pedigrees of your bitch or of the proposed stud dog.

HIP DYSPLASIA: Many breeders have their stud dogs X-rayed for HD, so they will have a certificate giving a hip score. When you are choosing a stud dog, you should ask to see the certificate.

A daughter of Ch. Tyegarth Famous Grouse, Onstage Grumble, pictured soon after producing a litter of seven puppies. It is essential that your bitch is sound in mind and body before breeding from her.

HEART CONDITIONS: For some time, it has been felt that the Boxer has been liable to heart problems. Sometimes youngsters faint while playing galloping games – but because they seem alright as soon as they get up, shake themselves and dash off again, little or no notice was taken, and it came to be called 'the Boxer Heart'!

In the last ten years this condition has been taken more seriously, particularly by the pet owners, who wanted to find out more about the problem. Dr Bruce Catternach, the Breed Council's Geneticist, agreed to set up sessions where a cardiologist could give official opinions on our Boxers. All over the UK these sessions took place, usually on the same days as dog shows, and any Boxer that was presented was tested. Now, some three years later, a picture is emerging which suggests that there are some serious heart problems in the Boxer breed. The Breed Council, on behalf of the Boxer Clubs, is collating lists of dogs who have been tested – those who have passed free from any murmurs, and those who have been referred to their vets for further investigation.

So this is another thing you will have to look into before embarking on breeding a litter. Get in touch with your local Boxer Club for information regarding a list of dogs who are free of heart problems, and search through your bitch's pedigree for any names which might be on the list. It is irresponsible for anyone to breed a Boxer litter from suspect lines.

BREEDING PROGRAMMES

There are basically three types of breeding programme to consider:

IN BREEDING: This is when two closely related dogs are bred together – mother to son, father to daughter or brother to sister. This should only be done if the breeder is very experienced and knows *everything* about the two dogs involved. The danger is that it can bring out faults in the dogs' ancestry, and it should not be done unless there is no other alternative.

LINE BREEDING: This is when family lines are mated together, such as cousins, or dogs that are even more distantly related. Often this method is used when a breeder wants to 'fix' a type or a particular attribute. Hopefully, you will get a couple of puppies in a litter with this attribute, and so you can incorporate it into future breeding programmes.

OUT CROSSING: This is when there is absolutely no family connection between the sire or the dam. It is a safe mating, but probably all the puppies will be slightly different. It can be useful if a breeder wants to introduce new blood into the kennel.

CHOOSING A STUD DOG

Having done your homework on your bitch and found that she and her family are free from any known hereditary defects, you can then choose a mate for her. You may get useful information from the breeder of your bitch as to which dogs might be suitable, or you may have seen a dog you like at a show. Your first consideration should be the look of the whole dog – each time you look at him, do you like him? Does he please you to look at? Does his front match his quarters, does he stand up and look noble? Next, and just as important, has he got a good character? Is he nice to know, nice to people and to other dogs?

If you are at a dog show you can have a look to see if there are any of his sons or daughters entered, and then you will have a chance to see what they look like. This is quite exciting homework and can be fun. Ask the owners of the dogs you like for stud cards or a pedigree, and ask for details about the dog and his character. Most people will be willing to talk about their dogs to anyone who is interested!

Colour is also a consideration. The inheritance of colour is pretty simple – if anything to do with inheritance is simple! Two brindles will produce a mixed coloured litter, brindle and fawn. The shade of colour can vary, either light or dark in both brindle and red/fawn. A pair of red or fawn Boxers will not produce a brindle puppy. To cause slight confusion, some brindles carry no red gene, and so they are dominant brindle.

White markings on puppies can follow the markings of either of the parents, and almost all Boxers, dogs and bitches, carry the white gene, so white markings are

RIGHT: Ch. Helderbrand's Jet Breaker: Winner of 21 Best in Shows, over 100 Working Groups and over 200 Best Of Breeds. It is essential to use a top-quality dog for breeding

BELOW: Breeders sometimes need to introduce new blood into their lines. Charles Walker of the Lynpine Boxers, imported the impressive Spanish Ch. Janos de Loermo of Lynpine.

common, and they can and will produce completely white Boxer puppies. Every fourth puppy can be born white, and statistics show that twenty-five per cent of puppies born are white. However, if either the mother or father is a solid colour, red or brindle, with absolutely no white markings (on the Continent it is thought black pads to the feet are essential), these Boxers are unlikely to carry the white gene, so cannot produce a white puppy.

I do not know what tests have been carried out on this particular colour problem, but the trouble is exacerbated by the fact that we like white marking on our Boxers, especially for the show ring. If we only mated solidly-coloured Boxers together, we might eventually be able to eradicate the white Boxer altogether. However, as the Boxer started off with a great deal of white ancestry, both in Bulldogs and Bullenbeisers, is this something we should aim for? I know that when I have to have baby white puppies put to sleep immediately after birth, I am devastated.

Any stud dog you choose should be in tip-top condition, and should have been used at stud before. I do not advise you to use the 'dog next door', however much you like him; he may not be efficient at the job you are asking him to do, and the mating might be exhausting for the dogs and come to nothing. It is better to use an experienced stud dog. Another thought which you might bear in mind is that if you use a Champion stud dog, this is quite a useful selling point, and the owner of the dog might be helpful when it comes to selling the puppies.

THE IN-SEASON BITCH

When your bitch comes into season, this is the time when she is able to conceive, and hopefully, nine weeks later she will produce puppies. A bitch can come into season for the first time from six months onwards, and she will continue to come into season for the rest of her life, unless she is spayed. Some bitches have regular seasons every six months, but others are not so regular. If you do want to breed from your bitch, you should mate her between the ninth and thirteenth day of her season – although I have known a bitch conceive on the third day of her season, and another produced puppies after being mated on the twenty-first day of her season. It is important to keep a check of your bitch's seasons, and this will help you to decide on the right time for mating. As a general guide, the 'fertile' period starts when the discharge changes from blood-red to straw-coloured. At this time the bitch will also be prepared to 'stand' for the dog. This can be tested by stroking her hindquarters, and if she is 'ready' she will usually move her tail to one side.

THE MATING

Consult the owner of the stud dog and decide where you want the mating to take place. It is usual for the bitch to go to the dog, but these arrangements can be changed for your convenience. If the dog comes to you, it is usual to offer to pay petrol expenses as well as the stud fee. The stud fee is paid as soon as the mating takes place, and, in some cases, two services are agreed for the same price. The second service should take place within forty-eight hours.

I do not advise letting a puppy go instead of a fee, as this means you cannot sell any puppies at all until the owner of the stud dog has taken his pick of the litter and this might be as late as eight weeks. The pick might be the one puppy you yourself wanted to keep, so you lose your choice of puppy in your own litter, and the owner of the dog will probably sell your puppy to a client and so you will lose touch with it completely. In fact, the owner of the stud dog can dictate the terms if you do not pay the full fee at the mating.

The stud dog owner should be experienced in supervising matings, and the owner of the bitch is usually only needed to hold the bitch steady during the mating and the tie. All dogs differ in their approach to mating; some go in for a lot of foreplay, other get straight on with the job. It is a good idea if the dog and the bitch have a chance to play together to begin with, and it will soon become clear if the bitch is ready for mating or not. When the dog has mounted the bitch, the tie takes place, although this is not essential for a successful mating. However, in most cases, the dog will dismount from the bitch and will turn so that he is standing back to back with the bitch. The tie can last for a few minutes or up to forty-five minutes, and you must make sure that the dogs are never left unsupervised at this time.

THE PREGNANCY

After the mating, you can sit back – except when you are exercising your hopefully pregnant bitch – and wait nine weeks, or any time between 57 and 72 days. Tell your vet that the mating has taken place and the date, so that he knows when the puppies are due. Keep your bitch well fed, and, more importantly, well exercised during the whole of her pregnancy.

It is advisable to speak to your vet before embarking on breeding a litter, as some vets have different ideas on caring for the brood bitch, and it is obviously preferable if your ideas coincide. For instance, there is a theory that the bitch should be wormed before mating in order to cut down on the amount of worms the puppies-to-be will have, so check on that. Another idea concerning worming is that if the bitch is given garlic during her whole pregnancy, this also cuts down on the worm burden carried by the puppies – one garlic pearl a day is all that is needed. Maybe these are old wives' tales, but I am sure that they work for some people, so they should not be dismissed out of hand.

The average pregnancy lasts for 63 days. It is easier to think of that length of time as nine weeks. However, puppies may be born as early as 57 days and do well, or as late as 72 days and be quite alright. In this case, it is only the owner who is utterly worn out with the waiting! During her pregnancy, a bitch may change very much in character – this may be the only way you will know that she has 'taken'. Some mothers-to-be become very affectionate, others become fussier and more demanding, some become hungrier. It may be better, in any case, at the later stages of a pregnancy, to feed three or even four times a day, although the total amount of food does not have to be increased. The food should, of course, be of the best quality, and some form of calcium might be given, although it is said that if the food is of good quality and varied, that is enough for the bitch herself to make the calcium for the puppies she is carrying.

One thing you should always bear in mind is that every pregnancy, and for that matter every whelping, is an event on its own, never like any other pregnancy or whelping that has happened before. Even with the same bitch, never mind if she has had several litters before this one, this next litter will be entirely different.

During her pregnancy, certainly during the later stages, your bitch may have a clean, clear silvery discharge. This is quite normal, and you should only be concerned if the discharge is coloured a greenish-yellow or a dirty thick pink. This is not a good sign, and so the vet should be informed. This clear silvery discharge will increase towards the end of the pregnancy, and may even form a clear string of discharge. This is the mucus which seals the cervix and when things start to happen, this starts to come away.

A few days before her due-date, you should introduce the bitch to her whelping quarters. You may have a specially manufactured whelping box – there are many good types on the market – or you may construct your own. It should be located somewhere warm and draught-free, and it should be big enough for the bitch to lie down comfortably, but not too big or the puppies could stray too far from their mother.

Chapter Twelve

WHELPING

THE FIRST STAGE OF LABOUR

Every whelping is different, and no matter how experienced you are, there is always something new to learn. I suggest that you read as much as you can on the subject before your bitch is due to whelp, and hopefully, you will be prepared for all eventualities. If you are a novice breeder, it is also a good idea to have a more experienced breeder you can call in, if necessary. Whatever your situation, it is essential that you have a good relationship with your vet, and if in doubt, seek expert advice without delay.

When whelping is imminent the bitch is on edge and becomes increasingly restless, constantly wanting to go out and relieve herself – in other words, she is cleaning herself out. At this time she may want to dig very violently in the garden, or in your best flower bed, so look out for your favourite plants! She may take to her whelping bed, scratching about and tearing the newspapers to shreds. This digging is probably a throwback to preparing a whelping bed of her own, safe and comfortable under a tree, or at the base of a hedge, where she can have her puppies away from the rest of the pack, and where they may be safe for a few days. I never discourage this, as I think this violent digging is excellent exercise for her at this time, and will get things on the way.

The bitch may also start panting and shivering, the shivering may be so violent that it almost borders on shuddering, and all the time she is turning round, to see what is going on behind her. This can be very difficult for her to do if she is large and full of puppies. But this is all part of the first stages of labour, so do not be too alarmed; stay with her to comfort her if she needs you – although many bitches pay no attention at all to anything but their own business, so leave well alone, but just be there.

Make contact with your veterinary practice at this time, so they know that things are on the move. You will have, of course, told your vet of the approximate date of the whelping, and they should now be told of the present situation. Your vet may ask about your bitch's temperature. I am usually so busy and anxious that I do not have time to take temperatures, and anyway I believe temperature may drop many hours, or even days before the puppies actually arrive, so maybe it is not all that reliable a sign. Refusing food is probably a more certain sign that puppies are imminent. A bitch often refuses food for about twelve hours before she is due, but I have had a bitch tuck into an enormous dinner, then produce a puppy a few minutes afterwards! That is what I mean about there being no hard and fast rules about whelping.

You should have plenty of newspapers available, as you will get through masses of papers during the whelping and afterwards. The base of the whelping box should have a very thick layer of paper, at least four whole newspapers thick, so that your bitch can shred them up and make a nest in them. You will need newspapers constantly while she is whelping, as you will want to remove the wet and soiled papers and replace these with clean dry papers, and you will need fresh bedding for mother and babies when the whelping is over.

Keep a look-out for the water bag appearing. This sometimes appears as a little balloon, which is part of the water bag. It may rupture all over the torn-up paper in the whelping box, soaking everything. Sometimes it bursts on your new carpet or on the best armchair or sofa – all these things have happened to me! Sometimes you may not see it at all; the bag may have ruptured in the garden, during the digging or when the bitch relieved herself. Do not worry about this, there is no puppy in this first bag; it just contains lubricants to make the passing of puppies easier. After that first bag has ruptured (amniotic sac) there should be a puppy within thirty to sixty minutes. Do not interfere at this stage, and do not try to help by puncturing the bag yourself. If your bitch wants to, she can rupture it herself by nipping or tearing it, and licking the liquid. Let nature take its course.

THE DELIVERY

Once the bag has ruptured, the bitch may start to contract. I always think there is something, probably some hormone, in the liquid from the water bag which starts off the contractions. In a Boxer, the contractions may be so slight at first that you may not notice them at all; you may just be aware that the rhythm of the bitch's breathing is slightly different. It is almost as if she is holding her breath now and again, and then going back to breathing normally.

As the contractions get stronger, the time she is holding her breath becomes more of a push, and this push can be quite strong and even violent and accompanied by grunting. Luckily, I have never had a bitch who cried or screamed when whelping, but I know that this can happen, and it must be very distressing to the owner.

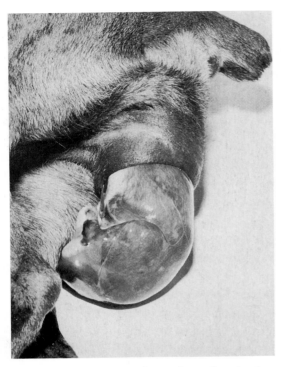

The puppy emerges from the vulva in the birth sac. In this instance the puppy is being delivered back feet and tail first.

It is important that the puppy breaks free from the sac as soon as it is delivered, so that it can start breathing. The bitch may break the sac or you may have to assist.

Some bitches like to stand when a puppy is to be born, others like to crouch, while others lie on their sides, and those which lie on their sides like to extend their back legs forwards as far as possible; some like to push against the sides or end of the whelping box. If your bitch likes to lie on her side to whelp, you may be able to see the progress of an unborn puppy moving upwards to be born. The flat part of the bitch's loin can be seen filling with the unborn pup, with one contraction. The puppy is moving upwards from the womb to the birth canal near her tail. With the next contraction, the bitch's tail will move slightly, and then her entire tail will be upright, which means that part of the puppy has entered the birth canal, and you may see a bulge appearing under her tail. There will then probably be a heave rather than a push, and the puppy's head may actually appear, and the whole puppy will then slide out and the mother will take charge.

Some puppies are born head first, while others are born back legs and tail first.

The bitch will lick the puppy to dry it, and to stimulate the puppy to breathe.

The placenta is attached to the puppy by the umbilical cord.

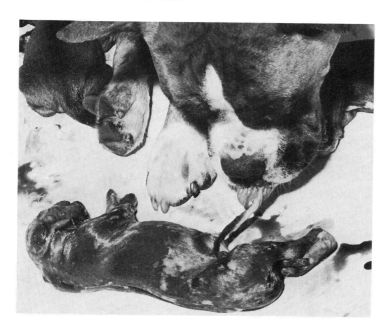

The bitch severs the umbilical cord. If she fails to do this, you may have to assist.

This tail-first presentation is not actually a breech birth, but it is known as a posterior presentation. In a breech birth, the back legs are tucked up under the body and are not stretched out with the tail, as in a posterior presentation. A head-first puppy may be born more quickly than one which is tail first, as the head of the puppy, being hard, engages in the birth canal, and that makes a strong contraction, so that the whole puppy can slide out quickly and easily. It is thought that as many puppies are born tail and back legs first as those that are born head first. A real breech birth and other different presentations sometimes slow up the whelping, but few actually need the help of the vet.

Puppies in a litter may be born at intervals of minutes or as long as an hour or so apart. The occasional pup is born alone after everyone thinks it is all over and have tidied up and gone to bed, and it is a lovely surprise in the morning! Often, after the first puppy is born, the mother cleans it over and over again, and she is so preoccupied that she does not get on with giving birth to any more. She will wait until the contractions start again, and she has to have the next puppy.

Each puppy is enclosed in its own bag. This bag is made of layers of very thick skin, and is full of fluid, it also contains the afterbirth (placenta). The whole packet, puppy, bag full of fluid and afterbirth usually come into the world together, at the same time. Occasionally the puppy appears on its own, with the membrane (the bag) still round it. Do not worry, the pup will still be alive, and as soon as the membrane is away from its head, it will be quite alright. You may have to help the mother to remove the membrane from the puppy, particularly over its head and mouth, so that it can take a first deep breath. The mother will start licking the pup vigorously and this will bring it to life, and then all will be well.

If the afterbirth does not come away with the puppy, it will probably come away on its own before the birth of the next puppy. At the final count of puppies, your vet may ask if all the afterbirths are accounted for. So it is as well to have had, or at least have seen, the same number of afterbirths as there are puppies. Every puppy has an afterbirth, but sometimes it is difficult to count them when a few puppies are born very quickly, only minutes apart. If the bitch deals with a newly born puppy by herself, she normally eats the membrane and the afterbirth. This does her no harm, in fact it contains valuable nutrients, although if she eats too many it may make her motions very loose for the next few days.

As soon as the mother has licked the new-born puppy, it should be placed on a teat so that it can start suckling. Some births are very wet, containing a great deal of fluid, others are drier with just the liquid from the first water bag and a small amount from each puppy bag. Unfortunately, there is no way of telling before the birth if it is going to be very wet or not. But if your bitch has a wet birth, there is no doubt that the whelping bed will be in a mess and many more newspapers to mop up will be needed. Whelping is a messy business. There may be a great deal of discharge from your bitch, but do not worry if it is dark-green as well as blood and clear liquid. The dark-green liquid is quite normal, although it does stain.

If there are any hold-ups during the whelping, or if your vet thinks that a puppy has been retained, a caesarian may be necessary. This is a veterinary decision, and so it is important that you have a good vet that you can trust. Puppies born by caesarian are often quite all right, just needing extra warmth. It is important to be there to reassure your bitch when she comes round from the anaesthetic, so that she accepts the newborn puppies and is prepared to feed them. However, within a couple of days puppies born by caesarian can be treated as normally born pups.

Whelping can last as long as thirty-six hours or it can be over in a couple of hours, depending on the number of puppies and the speed at which they are born. As soon as you think all is over, let your vet know that all is well. My vet makes a house call at the end of a whelping or immediately afterwards in order to check that all the whelps have been delivered, and to make sure there are no retained afterbirths. Some vets administer an antibiotic, just in case.

This is also a good opportunity for the vet to check the bitch's milk supply, and to see that the puppies are able to suckle and take milk from all the teats. It is important to check the teats every day in case there are any hard lumps which can turn into mastitis. Most Boxers have a very good supply of milk, and so it is essential that the teats are flowing freely. Your vet will show you how to make the initial check, and then it is just a matter of running your hands along your bitch's undercarriage every day to feel the mammary glands and ensure that all is well. If you detect any signs of hardness or lumpiness, get one of the large greedy pups to suckle from that teat. This might solve the problem, but you should consult your vet. If mastitis sets in, this is very uncomfortable for the bitch, and, at worst, it may mean that the bitch can no longer feed her puppies.

You will also want to make sure that the puppies are healthy. You or your vet must check that none of the pups has a cleft palate. In the early days of Boxer breeding this condition was quite prevalent, but fortunately it is not so much of a problem nowadays. You can check for it by putting a finger into each puppy's mouth, and you will be able to feel if there is anything abnormal. Cleft palates that occur with a harelip are easier to recognise. However, puppies that are born with a cleft palate or a harelip will not survive, so your vet should take them away and put them to sleep. They should not be kept in any case, as this malformation can be passed on. It is a lethal gene.

You may be unlucky to have white puppies or mainly white with just a bit of

Every fourth Boxer puppy can be born white, but a white Boxer cannot be entered for competition in the show ring.

colour somewhere. These were discouraged in the 1924 Standard, and so these pups should be put to sleep by your vet as early as possible. These whites are often large puppies who thrive, and nowadays some vets will not put them to sleep. It is possible to keep them, and the Kennel Club will register them, even when the Kennel Club Standard tells us "white markings acceptable not exceeding one third of ground colour". However, disposing of white puppies is a way of cutting down numbers in a large litter, so making things easier for the mother. It is quite possible that white puppies may be deaf, which can only be ascertained when the puppies are about eight weeks old, and then putting a puppy to sleep is quite soul-destroying.

Sound white pups are exactly the same as their coloured littermates, and it is possible to sell them, and they can make good pets. It is customary to sell white pups at half price, and so great care must be taken before any sale is made, to ensure that they go to good, permanent homes. They must not be discarded later as "no good". Many Rescue groups say that adult whites come into their hands far more than the coloured ones. The best homes for the whites I have found are those which want to replace a much-loved white Boxer. However, these homes are few and far between, and as a reputable Boxer breeder who is upholding the Boxer Standard, you should not want to keep white Boxers.

Chapter Thirteen

REARING A LITTER

THE FIRST DAYS

The first few days of a puppy's life are critical. I have found that if a puppy is going to die, it rarely survives longer than a couple of days. In other words, it has not really come to life properly. Of course, a great deal can be done at the time of birth to get a puppy breathing, such as vigorous rubbing with a warm, dry, rough towel, and then the bitch takes over, licking with a warm tongue, which is very therapeutic. But the odd puppy with some internal defect, which you cannot see, will usually fade away over the next few days. You may find it away from the others, dead in the corner of the whelping box. Sometimes the mother pays no attention to it at all, in fact she may have nuzzled it away from the rest of the litter. Something about the pup, maybe its urine, or just the smell of it, has told her that it is not worth bothering with, so it has been discarded. This may be very sad for you, having been with your bitch during her entire whelping. It seems such a waste of effort, but it is often the best thing in the long run, as you do not want to rear a sub-standard puppy, who may have some defect and will never make a vigorous companion.

Some years ago there was a condition called the 'fading puppy' syndrome, when newly born puppies just faded away, sometimes crying piteously, and crawling around aimlessly. Whatever you did, they just died off. One of my vets was very interested in this syndrome, and if I had a puppy in a litter which did not look very lively, there was nothing he would not do to keep it alive. A puppy with this syndrome feels frail, bird-like, and rather limp. One of my puppies had numerous injections in a bid to save it; we even set up a small oxygen tent, but the puppy did not survive. Antibiotics have now come to the aid of many of these poorly puppies.

HAND REARING

If your bitch has a large litter – anything over eight pups is large – you will need to help your bitch to feed them. There may be a couple of small puppies at the start, or, after the first few days, the small puppies are knocked off the teats by their bigger brothers or sisters. Consequently, they do not get as much milk and begin to look thin, and they fail to thrive. It is these puppies who need to be 'topped up' with extra rations, and this will also help the mother to cope.

Puppy or kitten feeding bottles can be obtained from your vet's surgery or from a good pet shop. Ask your vet what milk formula to use – he probably has a brand that he recommends. Many years ago, breeders made up their own formula, with sweetened condensed milk, egg yolk and glucose, and this also worked very well. To start bottle-feeding, pick the puppy out of the nest, and hold it in your hand. The milk should be warm (almost hot), and the teat should taste of milk when you put it into the puppy's mouth. A Boxer puppy needs a large-sized teat – teats for dolls' bottles are far too small. A dropper is much better in an emergency. Tube feeding is another excellent method of early feeding, but it must only be undertaken by a skilled, qualified person.

Make sure that each puppy you are supplementing takes about an ounce or so at a time. Some feed easily and well from the bottle, others do not take so much, but so long as the pup takes something it is a step in the right direction. After feeding, put the puppy back with the rest of the litter to fend for itself again. I reared a litter of ten puppies in this manner, topping up five pups in the morning, and then the other five (I hoped!) in the evening. The whole litter grew into big, happy, wild pups, and I found it a very rewarding experience. I had another puppy, who weighed only 8oz at birth – half the weight of the others in the litter. I topped up her feeding while she was a puppy, and although she never grew to full size, she produced several litters of full-sized puppies for me.

Observation is extremely important at all times in caring for dogs, and even more essential when rearing puppies. In fact, I believe that observation is the key ingredient in successful kennel management. Even if your bitch is a house pet, you should not undertake to breed a litter, unless you are willing to enter into this new, and more important branch of dog keeping. As soon as your bitch has whelped her first litter, you have become a dog breeder, and this involves a considerable amount of responsibility, particularly in relation to caring for your bitch and her puppies. So, after the first house visit from your vet to check the puppies, it is essential to observe the new 'family' at regular intervals every day. Then you will be able to spot any changes at the earliest possible opportunity.

In those first few days, you should take note of any signs of a change in the type of faeces, or a slightly different smell should immediately set you on your guard, and you should prepare yourself for possible trouble. As your Boxer bitch is a good mother, and is keeping her puppies scrupulously clean, signs of diarrhoea are very hard to spot early on; you may hear a puppy passing "squittery" motions. Any sign of yellow or green on the bedding or in the bed is a danger sign in very young puppies, and the results can be fatal. If you detect any signs of trouble, contact your vet.

When I am rearing a litter, I make sure that I have a supply of suitable bedding, and I find the pads made from specially developed polyester are the best for a nursing mother. It is heat-retaining and has excellent drainage qualities, so it is comfortable for both mother and puppies. It can be obtained from good pet shops and veterinary surgeries. You will need at least two or even three pieces for a Boxer litter. The whelping bed should be kept very warm. I use hot-water bottles, and these must be constantly refilled as they cool. After this first week, when I think a litter should be kept in a very warm, fuggy atmosphere, you may be able to relax a little, and allow the temperature to drop slightly. However, you must still be observant, watching out all the time for changes. Some of the changes you observe will be the normal signs of development, but other changes are dangerous and may require action taken to save further trouble. None of us want to rear sub-standard Boxer puppies.

The first week of life for puppies should be very still and quiet; the puppies just sleep and feed, (they feed almost all the time) and grow. I only weigh my puppies if they look different sizes. If there is a very small one, I weigh it, but if they look evenly matched, I do not worry about weights. A new-born Boxer puppy should be, and usually is, about 1lb in weight at birth, and just fits into your hand. In two weeks, if all is well, you will find it difficult to pick it up with one hand. If there is a huge pup, it will probably weigh 1 1/2 lbs at birth, but do not be surprised if, at eight weeks of age, all the puppies are the same size.

DOCKING AND DEWCLAWS

Docking is currently a very controversial matter. In Britain breeders can no longer carry out this operation, and vets must be called in. We can only wait and see whether docking is to be banned altogether, as has happened in some European countries. I have always relied on my vet to dock my puppies, and this is usually done early on, on the second day after birth. Dewclaws are also removed at the same time.

THE SECOND WEEK

By the second week, the puppies are just a little bit more active. They start to crawl, almost walking, using their legs. Keep them clean – the bedding and paper will need changing every day or every other day. In the middle of this second week, the workload increases, as the bedding and paper will need to be changed more often, sometimes twice a day if the litter is a large one. It is essential that the nursing bitch is kept on a diet of high-quality food, and she should be offered plenty of fluids. The amount she requires will depend on the size of the litter, but certainly, a well-fed bitch is the key to a contented litter.

Check the puppies' front feet every day, as their nails (claws) can grow long and sharp, and can hurt and damage the mother when feeding. Hold the puppy up to the light and cut off the very tip of the nail. This will need doing every day or two. At about eight or nine days old, the puppies' eyes start to open. At first there is just a chink, and within a day or two the whole eye opens. It is impossible to tell what the colour of the eye is going to be at this early stage.

THE THIRD EYELID

There has been a recent trend among breeders to try to sort out puppies in the nest by the colour of their third eyelids! At about ten days, when the eyes start to open, breeders try to detect whether the third eyelid is pigmented. The pigmented puppies are sold as show quality, while the others end up as family pets. This is certainly a novel way of sorting out good quality puppies from the rest, but in my opinion, it is ridiculous to concentrate on one single aspect, rather than assessing the puppy overall.

In the early 1960s I went to Holland and saw some marvellous Boxers. The ones I particularly liked were from the Cynodictia kennels, owned by To and Dick Onderwater. I was asked to go with the Onderwaters to Botrop in Germany, where Dick was to judge a Boxer Club Championship Show. It was very interesting for me, as a novice, to watch him judge. I was, however, a little puzzled at the end, when he had his bitch challenge line up, that he discarded a very nice Boxer, who had won a senior class.

On the journey home I asked him about this, and he seemed a little uncomfortable and then told me that the bitch had been operated on, so he felt that she was not worthy of top honour. I asked how did he know, and, after a little more probing, he said that the eye had been operated on. The third eyelid had been removed. What, he asked me, was the English Kennel Club's views on an operation to change the look of a dog? I did not know, but I was sure that the law-abiding British Boxer breeders would not stoop so low!

In 1966, Dick Onderwater came over here to judge the British Boxer Club Championship Show and I was to be in the ring stewarding for him. In the first class, he beckoned me over to look at the dog whose head he was going over; "Look, no third eyelid," he showed me, with a twinkle in his eye! I did look and was appalled.

Stainburndorf Xoanan, born in 1946, winner of four CCs, owned and campaigned by Mrs Elsie Ridley. A grandson of Frolich von Dom; a very nice-headed dog and a marvellous character. He had an unpigmented third eyelid, which some present-day novice breeders would regard as unsuitable for showing. An unpigmented third eyelid in one or both eyes is only unacceptable if it spoils the dog's expression.

Later in the year, I was judging an Open Show in the West of the country; I was delighted to have an entry of about 80. By this time I was very much aware of what a third eyelid was, and I was astounded to find that half the entry had one, or sometimes even two third-eyelids missing.

At that time, I was editing the BBC *News Letter* so I started an article in this News Letter: "Look into the corner of your Boxer's eyes ..." and described what the third eyelid was. I then wrote that I thought that to remove this membrane was a cosmetic operation and should not be done. A little later at a Championship Show, Marjorie Clemons asked me if I could show her what "that piece of skin in the corner of the eye looked like". I remember that we were standing in the benching marquee, so I turned to the first bench, looked carefully at the head of the dog on the bench – there was no third eyelid! I quickly went to another bench, where I found a Boxer with third eyelids, so was able to show Marjorie what I meant.

Since these two instances, I have always been very aware of third eyelids, and particularly third eyelids which have been removed. I wish breeders today would try to breed out the unpigmented third eyelid. This is difficult I know, but the unpigmented third eyelid is only a bit of white marking, which happens to be the skin in the corner of the eye. It would be easier to eliminate, if we were not so keen on flashy white markings. Unpigmented third eyelids are far less likely to be seen on plain black-faced Boxers, and there is nothing as nice as a Boxer with a lovely black face with expressive eyes. The only reason that an unpigmented third eyelid is unacceptable is if it spoils the expression. Anyway, the third eyelid should *never* be removed.

WEANING

At about three weeks, the puppies are up on their feet and starting to walk and some of them will bark. Bedding will require changing more frequently, and a week later the puppies will be playing with each other. At this stage, the hard work, for you – weaning – is about to start.

As you start weaning, you should also start worming your puppies – there is little point in introducing solid food just for the worms' benefit! All puppies are expected to be born with eggs of the worm inside them, so it is important to worm both the puppies and the mother, every week or ten days until you see stools free from worms. The mother has to be wormed as she has been cleaning up after the puppies.

As dog and cat worms can, in a few cases, cause illness and blindness in small children, it is very important that your pups are free from worm infestation. Discuss the worm problem with your vet, and he will give you advice, and tell you what medicine to use, and how to administer it to the puppies and their mother. Worming should continue until all your livestock is completely free from any sign of infestation. Remember that worm eggs cannot be seen and can hang about in the woodwork of the whelping bed, in bedding, or in the house.

As soon as the first dose of worming tablets or syrup has been given, weaning can start. This will probably be when the puppies are about four weeks old. At this time their teeth are just beginning to come through, and they are like needles! The mother is now leaving them more often, and for longer periods. The first solid food I give to puppies is best-quality lean raw meat, very finely minced. This must not come straight from the fridge; it must be slightly warmed to room heat.

The amount I offer each puppy is about the size of a walnut. I hold this in my hand, and with the puppy in the other arm, I offer it to the pup, sometimes easing the mince into the puppy's mouth. Some take it immediately, others are slower to catch on, licking at it and sucking it, and it sometimes takes two or three days to get them all eating the amount you want to give them. Don't worry, as soon as they really get the taste of raw meat you will be astonished at how quickly it goes down! In this way, you can be sure that each puppy gets the correct share of meat. For the first two days I feed raw mince once a day, and then I introduce a milky, cereal meal.

I mix a little milk formula, as directed, add a couple of spoonfuls of baby porridge,

A nice evenly matched litter of Skelder Boxer puppies, sired by Ch. Jenroy Pop My Cork To Walkon, bred by Joy Malcolm.

Puppies thrive on good food, fresh air, and the stimulation of lots of exciting things to explore. This litter is sired by Skelder Bonanza Boy out of Skelder Liquorice Stick.

Weaning is a time-consuming business, but it is not long before the puppies get the idea. This litter of seven bitches and five dogs, bred by Linda Carnaby, was sired by Ch. Jenroy Pop My Cork To Walkon out of Tartarian The Tarot.   *John Carnaby*

so it makes a thickish warm paste, and then I offer the dish to the pups. As they have always sucked milk from their mother, pups have to be taught to lap. They usually get their first taste by sucking the edge of the dish, but as long as they get something it does not matter at all. The first few days are utter murder – your lovely, clean pups become covered in milk and porridge, and they are only clean again when their mother goes in and does a cleaning-up job. However, by the beginning of the next week, you will find that the pups know all about the feeding business – nothing gets spilt and all dishes are licked spotless.

A slice of brown or white bread, soaked with milk or gravy, is another variation, but each time the food is changed, make sure that it does not upset the puppies. You will want to make a note of the feeding, what suits which puppy, so you can pass on that information to the new owners. Over the next week or so, introduce scrambled eggs for a meal, either with bread or biscuit or sponge cake, or the eggs might be hard-boiled and chopped up small. Cooked white fish, flaked small, is another alternative. It is a good idea to introduce good-quality puppy biscuit at an early stage, but avoid using any which includes dried meat, as I have found this makes puppies loose.

Try to establish a routine so that each puppy is fed separately at each meal, particularly the meat meal. When pups are fed together round the same bowl, I feel they are only eating to stop another one from getting the food, and when they go to their new home and are alone, they have no competition, and sometimes go off food and become difficult to feed. Another advantage is that in this way you can be sure how much each puppy is eating.

The only food I would advise you to avoid with young Boxer puppies is pork, especially bacon and ham. I do not feed these until the puppy is quite grown up. I do not advise using canned food, but that is up to you, and I must admit I know many well-grown, healthy Boxers, who have been brought up on this diet. Chicken is a useful food as an alternative, but do be careful of chicken and game bones. In fact, the only really safe bones are big marrow bones, either cooked or raw. Nowadays there are many excellent dry dog foods, containing all the additives necessary for dogs. I would recommend these both for pups and adult dogs, but be careful to stick to the instructions on the packages of proprietary brands. Do remember that these are all complete feeding formulas on their own, so nothing should be added. However, when feeding dogs on these dry feeds, a bowl of clean water must always be available. And remember too, that dogs do not have to change their diet as we do. If a method of feeding suits your dog, stick to it. Your dog will be quite happy to eat the same food every day, and will not require a change. In fact, a change in feeding might well upset your dog's stomach.

Gradually increase the amount of food given at each meal, also increasing the number of meals until the litter is getting four meals a day – first thing in the morning, in the middle of the day, early evening and last thing at night. You can give two meaty meals, one cooked meat, the other raw meat. Cooked chicken or cooked fish can alternate with the cooked meat, but I always think at least one meal a day should be raw meat. Offal or tripe can be given, and this should always be cooked.

Puppies will get more active as the time goes on, and will need toys to stimulate them. A small stone put into a screw top tin makes a good toy and will rattle and roll all over the place. The noise will drive you mad, but it is very entertaining for the puppies! They also like old empty cartons to tear up and play with, old tennis balls are excellent, but you should take care that they cannot tear off bits of rubber, as this could be dangerous if pieces were swallowed.

PROSPECTIVE PURCHASERS

People may want to come and see the puppies at this time, and most Boxer mothers are delighted to show off their family. It is important that children are well behaved, and they should not be allowed to pick up any of the pups, as a wriggling puppy is easy to drop and that may damage it. I do not mind puppies and children playing together, as the companionship is perfectly natural and very nice to see, but I do think that the puppies should be at least a couple of months old, and the children

FROM PUPPY TO CHAMPION

Norwatch Sunhawk Wanneroo (Ch. Fletcher of Sunhawk Norwatch – Ch. Sheffordian Ruby Tuesday of Norwatch) aged ten weeks.

Banks.

Norwatch Sunhawk Wanneroo, aged nine months.

Banks.

Ch. Norwatch Sunhawk Wanneroo, aged eighteen months.

Banks.

should be beyond the toddler age. Interviewing prospective new owners is another job you will have to do, and this must be done very carefully. Your beloved pups are going to be looked after and brought up by strangers. Few breeders like the idea of parting with their pups, but equally, few breeders want a pack of Boxers eating them out of house and home, and so good homes must be found. It is your responsibility to find a suitable home, and the task is made easier if you lay down some simple rules, and as gently and politely as you can, explain these to the prospective purchasers, and hope they adhere to them.

When a puppy goes to its new home, you should supply a detailed diet sheet, a list of dos and don'ts, initial training hints, dates of worming and type of medication given, and dates that inoculations should be given (or have been given). You can also give prospective owners details of local Boxer Clubs, and local dog training societies. You will need to supply a pedigree, plus Kennel Club registration forms. The price you ask for a Boxer puppy is difficult to fix. If this is your first litter, you may be advised to ask someone with more experience in the breed to come and assess the puppies. There is an old saying "that the price of a puppy is what you can get for it"! However, I think it is important to put the dog's interests first, and a loving family home comes top on my list of priorities.

Chapter Fourteen

HEALTH CARE

We are lucky that the Boxer is an athletic well-made breed, with a no-nonsense coat, and therefore it is relatively easy to care for. A good, well balanced diet, plus regular exercise should ensure that your Boxer stays fit and healthy, and hopefully, lives to a ripe old age. However, there are some common ailments, and a few hereditary conditions that the owner should be aware of.

ARTHRITIS: This can develop in middle to old age. Try and prevent your dog from lying around on cold or damp ground and getting cold. Consult your vet, as tablets can be prescribed.

BLOAT: This is a dangerous condition, and the key rules are correct feeding and careful observation. The stomach distends after a meal, and unless veterinary treatment is immediately available, this can prove fatal. I always feed my dogs twice a day, as two small meals pose less of a strain on the stomach than one large meal. Make sure that the biscuit is soaked with very hot water at least half an hour before feeding.

CHEYLETIELLA (CREEPING MANGE): This is a type of small parasite which burrows under the skin. It is commonly known as walking dandruff. The dandruff usually appears on the dog's back, but it can also be seen on other parts of the body. It is so small that it is hardly visible, and once under the skin it is very hard to detect. Careful treatment to remove the adults and the eggs from the dog is necessary to ensure that the long life-cycle is stopped. Cheyletiella can cause severe irritation to people, especially children and those with sensitive skins.

EAR MITES: During the summer your Boxer may pick up ear mites. These can also come from cats. Consult your vet, and ointment or ear drops will be prescribed.

EPILEPSY: This can be an inherited condition. Epileptic fits do not usually occur until a dog is twelve to eighteen months of age, and a fit may well occur when the dog is asleep. When the dog comes round, it is usually quite all right, but sometimes it is a bit bewildered. Make sure that the dog is protected from any dangerous situations while it is in a fit, and afterwards leave it in a quiet place to recover. In the older dog, fits do sometimes occur, and these are more likely to be caused by a brain tumour. In all cases of fits, veterinary advice should be sought, as these conditions can sometimes be helped by tranquillisers or anti-convulsants.

FLEAS AND LICE: During the summer your Boxer will probably come into contact with hedgehogs, and dogs with fleas and lice. Comb your dog once a week with a fine-tooth comb, and if you see any fleas or lice, get some spray from your vet or a pet shop, and apply as directed. Make sure that the dog's bed and blanket are also sprayed. In some cases, it is a good idea to bath your Boxer at the beginning of the summer with an insecticidal bath, which will keep him free from infestation for some time. Shows are an easy place to pick up fleas and lice, so if you are going to shows, particularly in the summer, make sure that you comb your dog regularly and thoroughly.

GROWTHS: Boxers are prone to lumps and bumps. If your dog develops a lump, consult your vet. Some are better left, others can be removed. Sometimes they can be tied off with cotton thread or a hair and they will wither away, others have to be cut out, but in all cases, see your vet about them.

HEART CONDITIONS: There is concern about the incidence of heart disease in Boxers. Aortic Stenosis appears to be particularly common, with Pulmonic Stenosis slightly less so. There may be a hereditary cause, so the Boxer Clubs, through the Boxer Breed Council, are organising heart surveys, where Boxers can be examined by veterinary surgeons who have a diploma or certificate in small-animal cardiology.

For further information, contact the secretary of your local Boxer Club, who can give you details of where these sessions are taking place. If you are planning to breed a litter, you must find out which dogs and bitches are affected, and those which are clear of any heart defects.

HIP DYSPLASIA (HD): This is a malformation of the hip joint. It is thought to be a hereditary condition, and it is made worse by dogs carrying too much weight, or by over-exercising growing puppies. In a mild form, it will not pose any problems for the average dog. However, if you are planning to breed a litter, you must ensure that hip scores are good for both dog and bitch. X-rays for HD cannot be taken until the dog is at least twelve months old (preferably eighteen months), as the bones are not formed before that.

INDIGESTION: I have already stated that the Boxer tummy is difficult, and you may well have a dog that suffers a bout of indigestion – sometimes referred to as 'hot tummy'. The dog will be uncomfortable and will not be able to settle; it will refuse food and drink. If the dog wants go out into the garden and eat grass, this should be allowed; it will probably make the dog sick, and then all will be well again. If the attacks continue, try changing the diet – complete feeds might be tried.

INTERDIGITAL CYSTS: Some Boxers are prone to these large, red lumps, which come up between the toes, usually on the front feet. They are very painful and until they burst the dog is most uncomfortable. Soak the foot in a jam-jar of salty water, as hot as the dog can bear, until the swelling goes down. If the cysts continue, consult your vet, as it is possible to get a vaccine made for the dog.

KENNEL COUGH: This is very contagious, and so it can cause big problems in a kennel. The affected dog coughs as though it has something in its throat, and will sometimes bring up froth. It may be caught from other dogs in kennels, or the dog can be infected by breathing in the virus, which is carried in airborne particles. This is similar to the way humans catch influenza or the common cold. A dog suffering from kennel cough should be isolated from the other dogs at once, kept warm and quiet, and prevented from running about. Your vet can administer antibiotics. This is not serious for most dogs, but it can be lethal for old dogs or young puppies.

LOOSE EYES: When a young Boxer is teething, the eyes sometimes show a lot of haw and redness, and the lower lid hangs down. If this occurs, ask your vet for some soothing eye ointment. Teething continues until the dog is about twelve months old, when the back teeth (molars) come through, and this may cause some discomfort to your dog. Never let your dog hang its head out of the car window when travelling. My dogs eyes have been adversely affected when driving near fields being sprayed, and sometimes the exhaust fumes can affect them. If you find that your dog persists in having loose eyes, check that there is nothing to cause an allergy in the house, such as new carpets and curtains, and be careful with the cleaning agents you use.

NETTLE RASH (ALLERGY): You may suddenly find that your Boxer has come up in large lumps. These are sometimes confined to its head, and sometimes they come up all over the dog's body, and they are very itchy. This can be caused by a dog running through nettles, but more often, it is caused by a change of food – even a different type of milk will cause it. Keep the dog quiet, and a dose of milk of magnesia cannot do any harm. If the bumps persist, see your vet, who will administer tablets or give an injection. Of course, whatever food you think may have caused the condition, should not be given again.

PROGRESSIVE AXONOPATHY (PA): PA is a disease affecting the nervous system. Although similar diseases are found in other breeds of dogs and another animals, this particular disease is only found in Boxers. PA is inherited, the mode of inheritance being that of a simple recessive gene, such as that for white puppies. Less then sixty cases have been identified since the disease was first recognised. Suspect cases (lacking veterinary diagnosis) have also been found, but remain few in number. PA, as a disease, has therefore never been a major breed problem.

However, the difficulty for the breed has been with the large number of clinically normal PA carriers. A scheme was drawn up by the Breed Council in 1981 to combat and control the spread of PA, and it was directed at the carrier animals. The control scheme remains in operation and should continue for several years to come. As far as pet owners are concerned it should be emphasised that firstly, the likelihood of an adult Boxer developing PA, whatever its ancestry, is negligible, and secondly, there is no reason why a possible carrier puppy, should not be a perfectly normal, healthy animal so long as the breeder has followed the Breed Council Control Scheme. Anybody who is considering buying a Boxer puppy, or breeding a litter, should obtain one of the Breed Council leaflets, either from the secretary of the Breed Council or from one of the Boxer breed clubs. The leaflet contains lists of dogs and bitches who are known carriers and a list of cleared dogs and bitches. Everybody connected with the Boxer must be eternally grateful to Dr B.M. Cattanach and the PA panel, who have worked so hard on this distressing disease.

SKELETAL SCURVY: This is acute pain and stiffness in the joints, usually in the legs. The joints feel hot to touch, and the dog is off-colour. Symptoms can start from ten weeks or up until ten months. Vitamin C, or ascorbic acid tablets, should be given while the puppy is young and should continue until the puppy is about one year old. Blackcurrant juice in the dog's water bowl can be tried.

STINGS: In the summer, a dog may get stung by a wasp or a bee. The sting is often on the mouth and the lip swells. Try to remove the sting, then apply a paste of bicarbonate of soda and water. Veterinary help may be needed if the sting and swelling is inside the mouth, affecting the tongue and throat. A sting on the nose may be dangerous, if it affects the breathing.

TEETHING: Puppies lose their baby teeth from three months onwards, and by about eight months they have got their second teeth. During this time the puppy may get swollen gums, flying ears and red droopy eyes, but these will improve once teething has finished. The puppy will want things to chew – leather objects like an old shoe are best. Large marrow bones are also good at this time.

TEMPERATURE: A dog's temperature should be 101.5F (38.6C), and it should be taken using a stubby-ended thermometer, kept solely for the dog. The thermometer should be inserted into the rectum about 1 1/2 in., for about one minute. This can be done with the dog standing up or lying down.

WORMS: ROUNDWORM: All dogs and puppies will have roundworms at some time. Puppies must be wormed at least two or three times before they go to their new homes. The first worming should be at three weeks, the second worming should be ten days later. The life cycle of the worm is fourteen days, so subsequent wormings must be done less than a fortnight apart. If the puppy is going to its new home where there are small children, extra care must be taken, and the new owners must contact their vet for a worming regime for the puppy, which must be strictly followed.
TAPEWORM: Adult dogs can get tapeworm, especially dogs that live in the country. Tapeworm are carried by rats and fleas. Segments can be seen in the dog's motion. See your vet at once, and he will give you tablets to expel them. All worming remedies purchased over the counter are unlikely to be so effective, and the old-fashioned methods may cause purging and discomfort. It is very important that all worming remedies are obtained from your vet.

OLD AGE AND EUTHANASIA: Old age for the Boxer is usually some time after ten years of age, but every Boxer varies. Some are old before their time, others seem to get younger all the time and never grow up. My bitch Feather is now eleven years old and behaves like the idiot she has always been – she scarcely has a white hair on her dark brindle coat, while Gracie, who is only seven years old, still behaves like a puppy, but her red coat is losing its colour, and the lovely jet black pigment on her muzzle is pure white so she looks very old.

When your Boxer starts to behave as though it feels old, you must take extra care of him. Exercise should be limited to what your dog is happy with, and feed small meals rather than over-burdening the stomach. Your Boxer may need to relieve itself more often, so be on the look-out for this. It is a good idea to take your elderly Boxer to the vet for a check-up, and this is a good opportunity to discuss euthanasia – well before you have to cope with the decision.

Unfortunately, dogs do not often die a natural death, peacefully at home. This has only happened to my dogs twice, and I have had many Boxers through my hands. Vets, nowadays, are very good and understanding about euthanasia, and dogs can be put to sleep very peacefully, and it is only us, the owners, who find it hard to cope.

When the time comes, try to arrange for the vet to call at your house, so your Boxer is not upset and feels comfortable in his own home – maybe he can lie in his bed, or on his favourite armchair, or a corner of the sofa. I am also afraid that you must ask your vet about the disposal of the body, so it is better to talk to your vet well in advance, when your dog is well and happy. It is possible to have an animal cremated, and the dog's name can be recorded and the ashes returned to the owner, if desired. These arrangements can be quite costly.

APPENDIX I

CANINE SOCIETIES

ATTIBOX: In every part of the world, there are Canine Societies and governing bodies for pedigree dogs. In Europe this is the FCI, which is based in Belgium. For Boxers, the governing body is Attibox, who control all Boxers and Boxer events in Europe. This does not apply to the UK, because of quarantine regulations, which means that no dogs from the UK can compete on the Continent. However, people can take part, so on occasions delegates from the United Kingdom have attended meetings of Attibox, which take place yearly, often coinciding with the Attibox annual show, which is held in a different country each year. If changes gradually creep in to the shape and character of the Boxer, these changes are discussed and, if detrimental to the breed, judges and breeders can be instructed to take steps to eliminate these changes or faults. I have been privileged to attend two of these meetings, and although they were not held in English, they were very interesting, and the UK delegates were made very welcome. Some years ago, when Peggy Haslam and Marion Fairbrother went to one of these meetings, they thought it would be a good idea to have an organisation such as Attibox over here, and as a result the Boxer Breed Council was formed.

BOXER BREED COUNCIL: Every Boxer club in the United Kingdom is affiliated to the Breed Council. They send two delegates, who are instructed by their Breed Club. Matters concerning Boxers and administration of the breed are discussed and decisions taken. The Breed Council choose a representative to attend the meetings of the Kennel Club Liaison Council. The Council collates the dates of Club Shows to avoid clashes, and is also responsible for keeping a list of breed judges, based upon their experience in the breed and their judging record. An "A" List comprises those who have awarded Challenge Certificates.

ENGLISH KENNEL CLUB: This EKC administers to all pedigree dogs in the UK. This Club is in London, and consists of a social club, as well as administering to all dog clubs and overseeing all regulations concerning pedigree dogs, licensing every dog show, and obedience show in the UK. Anyone who judges a dog show has to be approved by the Kennel Club. Any pedigree dog or bitch can be registered at the Club; no unregistered animal can be shown at a licenced show. The Kennel Club approve and have the copyright of every Standard of each breed. The Club organise and are responsible for the running of Crufts Dog Show. There is an excellent Kennel Club Library, which is open every day to the general public during office hours, and is extremely useful for looking up records etc.

AMERICAN KENNEL CLUB: In America, the governing body for pedigree dogs is the American Kennel Club, who instigated the Good Citizen Scheme. The American Boxer Club is based in the New York area, and is the senior Boxer Club, but there are Boxer Clubs in most States and large towns. Boxer shows take place all over America including Hawaii.

AUSTRALIA AND NEW ZEALAND: There is a governing body for pedigree dogs, but each State has its own rules and regulations. There are Boxer Clubs all over the country and Canine Societies in and around each large city. The number of Boxers entered at these shows is not large, so it is possible to make a dog into a Champion in a very short time without travelling very far. Entries are more numerous at the Royal Shows and Club Shows, but to travel Inter State to Club Shows can sometimes take days. This also applies to New Zealand, to some extent, and travel from North to South Island usually requires a flight.

APPENDIX II

BIBLIOGRAPHY

British Boxer Club Record Book Vol 1.
British Boxer Club Record Book Vol 11.
British Boxer Club Year Book.s
American Boxer Club Anniversary Albums.
All About The Boxer, John Gordon. Pelham Books.
Il Boxer, Franco Bonetti. Editoriale Olimpia.
Judging The Boxer, Enno Meyer, Orange Judd Publishing Co.
Boxerliebhaber, Verlag Boxer-Club EV.
The Boxer Handbook, Joan Dunkles.
The Boxer, Elizabeth Somerfield. Popular Dogs.
My Life With Boxers, Friederun Stockmann.
The Boxer, J. P. Wagner.
Boxers, Constance and Wilson Wiley. Foyles.
The Book of the Bitch, J.M. Evans and Kay White. Henston.
Dogs And How To Breed Them, Hilary Harmar. Gifford.
The Boxer, MacDonald Daly. W. & R. Chambers.
De Boxer, Jan Van Rheenen.
Boxer Blarney, Marion Fairbrother and Peggy Thomson. New Lythe.
Save Our Dogs, Dr Ian Macadam.
Scrapbooks lent by Millicent Ingram with *Our Dogs* and *Dog World* Boxer Breed Notes going back to the 1930s.

THE WORLD FAMOUS
MARBELTON BOXERS

proudly presents the kennel's 22nd British Champion, namely
CH. MARBELTON OOH-LA-LA
(right), pictured with her litter sister,
MARBELTON EVERY INCH A LADY (1 CC).

They are sired by **MARBELTON OZONE FRIENDLY** (1 CC, 2 Res. CCs) out of
CH. LOOK NO FURTHER AT MARBELTON.
We usually have top quality puppies for sale and can offer top quality dogs at stud. Mary's books, *I WISH I HAD A CHAMPION*, can be purchased from this address at £14.95 plus postage.

MARY & JOHN HAMBLETON,
Marbelton Boxers, Gaw Hill Lane, Aughton, Lancs. L39 7HA.
Tel: 0695 422261   Fax: 0695 423279